As Evil Does

For Rita

Fred Harrison's previous publications include

The Traumatised Society (2012)
Ricardo's Law (2006)
Boom Bust (2005)
Power in the Land (1983)

Fred Harrison's blogs are on
www.sharetherents.org

His videos are on
www.youtube.com/user/geophilos

Twitter: **@geophilos**

For a full list of Fred Harrison's publications, go to
http://www.shepheard-walwyn.co.uk/authors/fred-harrison/

Handbook on Humanity 1:
Anatomy of a Killing Cult

As Evil Does

Fred Harrison

*Geo*philos

The right of Fred Harrison to be identified as the author of this
work has been asserted by him in accordance with the Copyright
Designs and Patents Act 1988

First published in 2015 by
Geophilos
7 Kings Road
Teddington,
TW11 OQB, UK

British Library Cataloguing in Publication Data
A catalogue record of this book is available
From the British Library

ISBN 978-0-9933398-0-6

Designed by Ian Kirkwood design
www.ik-design.co.uk

Printed by IngramSpark

Contents

Prologue: Between Good and Evil   1

Part I
Messing with our Minds
Chapter 1   On Happiness and Civil War   13
Chapter 2   Survival of the Unfit   23
Chapter 3   'Not Cheating? Not Trying!'   35

Part II
Cultural Cannibalism
Chapter 4   Cheating as Social Process   51
Chapter 5   Of Zombies and Zealots   65
Chapter 6   The Killing Cult   79
Chapter 7   The Con in Convergence   93

Part III
Outsmarting Evil
Chapter 8   Lairds, Looters and Pots of Gold   107
Chapter 9   The New Financial Architecture   121
Chapter 10   A Unified Theory of Humanity   133

Epilogue: Beyond Democracy   143

Appendix: Mortgaging Your Life   153

Index   155

Acknowledgements

Faced with the daily reminder of the unremitting evil that abounds in our world, it is crucial never to lose sight of the streak of decency in the human spirit. I am reminded of what is good in humanity by the dedication of the corps of campaigners for justice around the world who have worked with me for what has now become a lifetime of activism. On this occasion, I wish to extend special thanks to Mason Gaffney, Ron Banks and Anthony Werner; and colleagues at the Land Research Trust – Nicholas Dennys, Peter Smith and Mark Wadsworth. Ian Kirkwood was generous in offering his skills at converting my amateur images into professional graphics. My daughter Nina added to my understanding of the human condition in the realm of psychology. Rita, my wife, served as editor. I cannot express in words the debt I owe her, as a witness to the capacity of humans to overcome evil.

Prologue

Between Good and Evil

HITLER'S Luftwaffe arrived over the Houses of Parliament on the night of May 10, 1941. The bombs destroyed the House of Commons. Winston Churchill survived to oversee the reconstruction of the building that symbolised Britain's political system. In the debate on how to replace the structure, he used a phrase which serves as a metaphor for the thesis in this book. Churchill declared: "We shape our buildings, and afterwards our buildings shape us". Churchill was alluding to more than the stone, bricks and mortar of the physical structure. The building was an institution. When the architects first visualised the design, they did so with a purpose. The external edifice had to emboss an indelible impression on the minds of the population. The contours of the corridors had to channel the law-makers into accommodating what I called (in *The Traumatised Society*) the culture of cheating. The cultural architects, in a step-by-step process over a protracted period, designed the building to serve their private interests. Having completed the structure, they could sit back and safely assume that "afterwards our buildings shape us" – meaning, everyone else would (by hook or by crook) conform to their interests. And so it has been.

The first brick in the cultural edifice was laid 800 years ago. This took the form of a negotiation in the fields outside Windsor Castle, on the banks of the Thames. The barons and knights, whether conscious of it or not, were entering into an apprenticeship. They and their sons would be the architects of a new kind of kingdom. They signed a deal which, yes, gave us *Habeas Corpus*. But as the indentured manipulators of the common rights of the people of England, they took the first step towards a financial system which became the organising principle for the propagation of an evil that blights people's lives today. That organising principle became the artificial intelligence that overwhelmed the innate, organic intelligence that informs the authentic culture of free people.

In Magna Carta, the king – who was supposed to represent the welfare of all of his subjects – agreed to change what looked like a small detail in the financial arrangements of his domain. Sir Kenneth Jupp, who for 15 years served as a judge in the English High Court, interrogated that clause.

1

At about the time when Churchill was pondering what to do about the flattened Commons, Kenneth Jupp was busy earning the Military Cross for heroism on the field of combat against the Nazis. Later in life, he reflected on the history of the British legal system. He concluded that in the decade following the signing of Magna Carta in the fields of Runnymede "the main burden of government expenses was shifted from land to personal property, and hence to the whole population except the very poorest, without any regard to their holding of land".[1] From then on, the unremitting shift in the structure of the State's finances institutionalised the cheating which today manifests itself in a thousand and one ways. That anti-social transformation of the nation's finances was validated by the Parliament that meets in Westminster.

The people of England did not give their consent to the elaborate design that went into what became the building on the banks of the Thames. Even its name – the House of Commons – was calculated to manipulate people's minds. That house served a culture which abused the people of the commons of England, and then of the British Isles, for centuries. The ethos was fashioned by a small minority (the feudal nobility) to privilege their class. And so, now, that House shapes our lives in ways which defeat our best personal and social interests. Has the time come to reshape the building? Coincidentally, the structure itself is crumbling. Rehabilitation will cost up to £7 billion to shore up the walls and reconfigure the corridors of power. Is this not the timely occasion for a national conversation about the principles which should inform the redesign of Parliament? A conversation that engages everyone in the disunited kingdom?

The peoples of all four nations of the UK have registered their dissatisfaction with the political elites. This is the only construction that can be put on the outcomes of the general elections of 2010 and 2015. No one political party was given a mandate to govern – if, by mandate, we mean the electoral support of the majority of voters. But that raises the problem which is at the centre of the political and philosophical crisis which afflicts Britain. That crisis was neatly articulated by David Marquand, an acute observer of British social history in his various roles as Member of Parliament, head of an Oxford college and Chief Advisor in the Secretariat General of the European Commission. In *Mammon's Kingdom*, he noted that a large majority of the British people were trapped. They would "dearly love to escape, but *we don't know how to*. Instead, we thrash around in dumb despair. I believe we can spring the trap if we put our minds to it".[2]

What was it that had reduced to dumb despair a population which places a premium on reason and science? What could trap the people whose inventive genius produced the technologies which made mass production possible? These people, we must remind ourselves, gave the modern world some of the most distinguished philosophers. To decode the malevolent process that closed

---

1 Kenneth Jupp (1997), *Stealing our Land: The Law, Rent & Taxation*, London: Vindex, p.67.
2 David Marquand (2015), *Mammon's Kingdom*, London: Penguin, p.xxi. Emphasis added.

their minds to *knowledge that was known to their ancestors*, we need to confront a painful reality.

The tragic condition of Britain today is primarily the result of the violent rupture of the people from the material embodiment of their humanity. *We have been systematically dehumanised.* The disturbing (not to say painful) implications of that proposition invites denial. And so I am obliged to provide conclusive evidence. Part 1 of this volume considers whether the language and narratives we employ are reliable guides to reality. If not, that establishes the need to question the origins of Anglo-centric civilisation. Like the earliest anthropologists of the 19th century who had to hone new analytical tools so that they could interrogate the remains of pre-historical societies, we also need to refine our conceptual equipment. This we do in Part II in the course of assembling the apparently relevant facts. In Part III, we evaluate the facts to determine whether we have it in ourselves to chart a new course for humanity.

Our intent is to excavate the motivating logic in the structure of the social system. The crises that we have to endure are so repetitive that they cannot be random events. Are the social pathologies we endure *necessary legacies* of the culture we have inherited? If so, they will continue to plague us unless we identify their source(s). Today, most explanations are sought in events that have happened in the last 40 years or so. Thus, the widening gap in incomes is attributed to something vaguely denoted as "globalisation". Might the cause of such traumas be rooted in the distant past? But rooted in what, exactly? Politicians play *ad nauseam* with palliatives. Something inhibits them from employing policies with the power to resolve our social problems. If we want the cure we need to name the cause.

Evil in our midst

The evil which stalks Britain today does not originate in the realm of the supernatural. Again, for illumination we cannot do better than the words of Winston Churchill, this time in a speech he delivered in Edinburgh in 1909. For him, evil denoted that which blighted people's lives.

> "We see the evil, we see the imposture upon the public, and we see the consequences in crowded slums, in hampered commerce, in distorted or restricted development, and in congested centres of population... "[3]

These were not random symptoms in an otherwise Good Life. By evil, Churchill meant the systematic way in which the distribution of income was rigged to discriminate against the welfare of the population. He saw how one class benefitted from that discrimination: the owners of land. That was why, as a Liberal Member of Parliament, he campaigned to reform the tax system. He

---

3 Budget League (1910), *The Budget The Land and The People*, 4th edn., London: Methuen, p.53.

wanted new charges on the rents that flowed into the pockets of land owners. If Churchill and his comrade-at-arms, the Welshman David Lloyd George, had succeeded in reforming High Finance, the people of Britain would have embarked along a different route through the 20th century. Evil in its institutionalised forms would have been expunged from the fabric of society. *Really?* Can we place such a burden on a simple redesign of the way government raises its revenue? I will demonstrate beyond doubt that, yes, we can. Unfortunately, the people of Britain were denied the opportunity to prove the correctness of this proposition. They were prevented from reclaiming their ancient rights. How and why this happened tells us all we need to know about the building in Westminster, whose design has successfully distorted our lives.

At the end of the 19th century and, for the first time in their history, a representative majority of the people of Britain were free to give their consent to a revised form of governance. Through their votes, they granted a democratic mandate for the reform of taxation. Their political will was embodied in what became known as The People's Budget of 1909. However, landlords in Parliament fought a rearguard action in the courts, buying the time so that events might overwhelm the will of the people. The budget's key clauses, on taxing the rents of natural resources, were not implemented. Evil triumphed.

Is it now possible to re-launch Churchill's mission to abolish that evil? Governments have the antidote, but they refuse to apply it. The nation is trapped in limbo land, between good and evil. But if the politicians are inhibited, what gags the conversation in civil society? Could it be that the collective consciousness of the people has been so damaged as to impair an informed debate? Marquand argues that people can apply their minds to the problem. This, in my view, is subject to a proviso: *only if they have the information that exposes the reasons for their dehumanisation.* And that entails a clear understanding of the significance of that income called *economic rent*, to which Churchill drew attention a century ago.

Rent is here used in a specialised sense. It is not the sum paid by tenants who lease apartments, or by motorists who hire cars. To define the concept, we will borrow the words of Alfred Marshall (1842–1924), one of Britain's greatest modern economists. He was the theoretical bridge between classical economics and the post-classical schools of the 20th century. In the 8th edition of *Principles of Economics*, published in 1930, he explained (on page 433) that what was commonly called the "original value" or "inherent value" of land should more correctly be called *"public value"* (Marshall's emphasis). Marshall focused on the services that originate in nature. These are provided without cost to us. But it is important to bear in mind that rent is a composite value. It also includes the value of services that are provided by society.

To fully appreciate the distinctive nature of this public value, we need to locate its significance in terms of human evolution. By incorporating that dimension, we inspire awareness of the terrible crime that was committed by the aristocrats who first separated the people of England from that stream of income.

Rent is the material embodiment of our humanity. It is that quantum of energy produced by morality and social solidarity. For practical purposes, it can be measured and allocated in a variety of ways – in physical goods (such as food or raw commodities) in a barter economy; or in cash terms, in a complex market economy. But its essence is humanity itself. The moral sentiments of early humans evolved organically, intuitively, alongside the rules and rituals that nurtured social solidarity. These were nourished by the biological bonds that were expressed through love, and the social bonds that were expressed through trust. These qualities achieved a material form: the resources that people willingly reserved for the common good. Today, we call those resources rent. Rent was – and remains – the sacred income. Without it, the common good is starved, and we are collectively degraded, no longer able to act as fully conscious, paid up human beings.

To realise our potential as humans, we have to accept responsibility for our actions. But isolated individuals cannot meet their responsibilities if their communities have been disabled, incapable of accepting responsibility for what goes on in the public domain. That is the tragedy of the human condition today. *The virus of greed now controls all the levers in the junction boxes of those institutions that are supposed to serve the common good.*

▶ The culture of cheating evolved the capacity to shroud in mystery the social nature of rent; the size of that flow of revenue within the nation's income; and the manner in which its privatisation damages our lives.

From this it should follow that

▶ if we transform the tax regime so that it serves everyone's best private and social interests, cheating *as an institutionalised process* would be terminated. It can survive only for so long as rents are privately appropriated.

But is it true, that the status of rent is concealed from us? Isn't ours an "open society" in which information is freely exchanged? I will explain how, in relation to this one stream of income, strenuous efforts are continuously made to close our minds to the material basis of the common good. If that claim is correct, it raises painful issues about the state of society and our collective mental health. An illustrative example of the problem is a book which recently made one economist a superstar in the academic firmament. In a volume of 685 pages, his treatment of rent amounts to just two full pages. And for good measure, he brands this "The Mystery of Land Values".[4]

There is no mystery about rent. If we are to outsmart evil, one of our tasks is to understand why most economists claim that mystery surrounds that stream of income. But to achieve the required clarity of thought, we must first reconcile ourselves to the psychotic state of modern society.

---

4 Thomas Piketty (2014), *Capital in the 21st Century*, Cambridge, Mass: Belknap Press, p.196.

Is ours a psychotic society? Such a proposition offends our default position: that we are all "normal" except for the psychopaths who ought to be behind bars.

Psychosis is defined as

"...a chronic mental state characterised by loss of contact with reality, disorganised speech and behaviour, and often by hallucinations or delusions."

If this is a robust description of the human condition, we begin to sense the forces that deprive us of the happiness we all seek. So a further task is to recover a sense of reality. To aid us, we need the guidance of a model of how our world, in its current state, actually works. But if we are collectively locked into a psychotic state, how can we recognise a healthy state of affairs? With difficulty. That is why we need to engage in cleaning up our language. Then we can differentiate delusion from reality.

The Commons in action

What does a healthy culture look like? To qualify as an authentic representation of humanity, culture has to ensure harmony and continuity in people's lives. It has to provide the tools with which to minimise risks, cope with unexpected challenges, and empower people to work at achieving their aspirations. How does a healthy culture facilitate these goals?

Culture that is life-enriching accommodates biology's building blocks. Our shared gene pool endows individuals with the capacity to procreate in extended family and social units. To facilitate social evolution, culture has to endow each generation with the capacity to produce the wealth that fulfils both personal and social needs. But we are more than material creatures. Culture achieves its aesthetically exquisite expression through art and sculpture, and through the rich variety of physical representations of the ideas in our minds. Those ideas coalesce in the rules which represent the values that we call morality.

All of these qualities constitute the commons, the shared endowment that a healthy society bestows upon each new-born child. Induction of each child into the commons is the process of affirming and sustaining humanity.

The commons is the complex nexus of qualities that define relationships in all their forms. These find their practical expression in the formation of the personality of each and every individual. The relationships are schematically traced in the graphic.

▶ *Spatial regulations* guide our relationship to the natural world. Stewardship of the land that we need to sustain our material existence secures our biological survival.

▶ *Culture* enhances our shared wellbeing. Society nurtures the collective consciousness and embodies the institutions that enable us to go about our daily business.

▶ *Values* are the foundation of the trust that is needed for psychological health, and for the integration of the individual into the caring community.

We are individuals, yes, but first and foremost we are composites of the commons. Individuality is measured and celebrated by the degree to which it stands out from that which we share in common.

That part of personality which we share in common emerged in, and is continuously enriched through, the complex interaction of the triadic relationship that constitutes the commons. Humanity is defined by the commons. Humanity grows as the commons expand. That is why, in return for what is received at birth, the individual makes a personal contribution to the further enrichment of the commons. This mutually beneficial arrangement delivers ever richer lives for each succeeding generation.

▶ *Natural habitats* yield ever more munificent bounties with every leap forward in the evolution of our species

▶ *Institutions and rules* combine in ever greater sophistication to deliver the enhanced use of labour and capital resources

▶ *Moral codes* grow richer to emancipate populations in ways that deepen the individual personality and possibilities

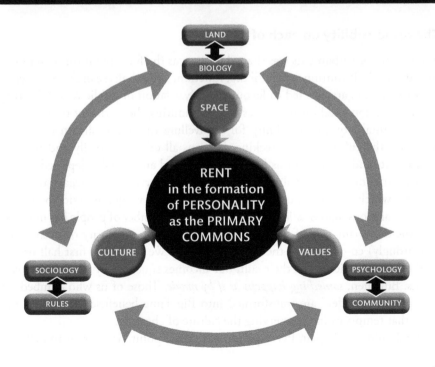

The formation of personality

LAND
BIOLOGY
SPACE

RENT
in the formation
of PERSONALITY
as the PRIMARY
COMMONS

CULTURE
VALUES

SOCIOLOGY
RULES

PSYCHOLOGY
COMMUNITY

The feedback loops within this dynamic process are sustained by the continuous circulation of the energy that each person contributes to the wellbeing of the whole. That energy takes the form of the rent that we all help to produce. Rent is the material life-force that nourishes our humanity.

The architectural spirit that guided humane forms of culture embedded rent into the edifice in ways which delivered self-perpetuating motion and willing adherence by successive generations. The logic in this structure of culture serves as innate intelligence. It ensures both stability and, where appropriate, the capacity to adapt to new ways of thinking and behaving.

The severest threats to humanity, and to personal wellbeing, arise when any one part of the commons ceases to work in harmony with the other parts of the system. That implies that the innate intelligence networks are malfunctioning. The greatest dislocations arise when rents are diverted out of the interlocking system. As that energy haemorrhages away, the social immune system is weakened, exposing everyone to mortal risks.

To make convincing this broad outline of the nature of humanity, and the conditions for its continued existence, the evidence will be presented in a trilogy. Volume 1 treats the United Kingdom as the case study for a forensic examination of what happens when people are ruptured from their natural and social habitats. Volume 2 tests the evidence by investigating the fate of previous civilisations, to determine whether Europe faces an existential threat to its survival. Volume 3 addresses the nature of secular power to assess whether we need the intervention of spiritual force to solve problems that defeat current forms of governance.

The responsibility on each of us

The Mother of Parliaments was shaped to serve as the focal point for manipulating our minds. It continues to fulfil that function, as we shall see in the persistence with which laws are enacted to favour the privatisation of public rent. Cheating in its institutionalised form survives by dishonouring the norms of transparency and accountability. Responsibility for unravelling this mess falls on every one of us, for the culture of rent-seeking demeans all of us spiritually and psychologically. It renders many of us financially indebted and socially deprived, and it impoverishes our natural habitats. Our children deserve a better legacy than the one into which their parents were inducted. What are we going to do about it?

The avaricious, narcissistic inclinations of a tiny number of people has mutated into the dominant way of life in the 21st century. The majority of us are now (unwittingly) co-opted into the culture of greed. We spend the first half of our working lives as victims of their cult, our incomes squeezed by mortgage repayments. But then, *something happens as if by magic*. Those of us who climbed on "the property ladder" are transformed into Big Time beneficiaries. That is the bribe that tempts us into preserving the culture of cheating.

We should not despair. Every person is a power point. The power to make or break. The power to love or hate. If we resolve to act as socially responsible beings, united to re-create rather than carve up our communities, we can re-orientate our minds and restore to working order humanity's moral compass. The first step is to engage in a national debate. That engagement becomes the therapeutic process which liberates our minds. Out of that conversation would emerge a consensus that may once again lead the people of Britain to mandate the democratisation of the public's finances, which is nothing less than the restoration of our humanity.

In every cry of every Man,
In every Infant's cry of fear,
In every voice: in every ban,
The mind-forged manacles I hear.

WILLIAM BLAKE, *London*

Part I

Messing with Our Minds

1

On Happiness and Civil War

H IS SECRET haunted the Director of the Bank of England for 50 years. A secret that he took to his grave. So terrible was the knowledge that it had to be concealed for fear of causing a civil war.

George Warde Norman had discovered the financial algorithm that would deliver happiness.

He worked out the formula in his early years, and he began to commit it to paper in 1821. Over the following decades he extracted the script from his bureau to strengthen the case with yet more empirical evidence. As he helped to shape the financial future of the world's first industrial power he probed tirelessly into what he called the "evil" that afflicted the nation. But he could not bring himself to share the antidote to that evil with the people of the United Kingdom.

He kept the manuscript under lock-and-key in his ancestral home outside London, in the town where he chaired the committee that administered the Poor Law for the destitute.

Norman was a paid-up member of the British Establishment. He was educated at Eton College, was an intimate of the influential London circle of intellectuals that included biologist Charles Darwin and philosopher John Stuart Mill, and a confidant of the most powerful people in government. He inherited a fortune in the form of houses, land and money worth, in 2009 values, £17m. This made it possible for him to relax and reflect on the problems of the day. He enjoyed open access to HM Treasury, where at one point he was adviser to the Chancellor of the Exchequer. There was no shortage of opportunities to influence the nation's policy-makers: on more than one occasion he attended parliamentary commit-tees as a witness. George Warde Norman had the opportunity to influence the destiny of a rapidly-changing society. All he had to do was divulge his secret.

Norman's quest for the secret of happiness stemmed from his support for the Utilitarian philosophy elaborated by Jeremy Bentham (1748-1832). At the heart of this doctrine was the idea that society was obliged to achieve the greatest hap-piness for the greatest number of people. Bentham invented a "felicific calculus" to add up those actions which, in his view, would deliver that happiness. Norman was not convinced. And so, he set out to discover happiness through financial reform. In his manuscript, he "formulates a sort of legislator's guide, a set of criteria which should be used in achieving the Utilitarian goal. It should be used in evaluating existing taxation, and it should act as a guide to those imposing taxes".[1]

His findings weighed heavily on his conscience. He wrestled with the need to publish the results of his research, but in the end he chose self-censorship.

Norman feared that, if attempts were made to implement his plan, it would "occasion commotions and civil war". The financial algorithm for happiness was incendiary.

What was so harrowing about that formula that persuaded him to sacrifice the happiness of the people of Britain? That there was a need for more happiness, no-one could doubt. The population was divided into adversarial classes, children forced to earn their living by climbing up the insides of chimney stacks, men worn down to premature death in factories. The people whose ingenuity, hard work and sacrifices had blazed the trail to mass production had earned the right to happiness.

The code that Norman had managed to break was the Holy Grail of good governance. He had worked out how to liberate people to achieve prosperity without prejudicing the rights of others. This is what he recorded in his *Autobiography*, which he also decided not to publish:

> "If people could only be found to agree with me in feeling – but that they never will do, and it is probable that an attempt to establish one sole Tax in England, or France, would infallibly fail, and if persisted in, occasion Commotions and civil war... My *Essay on Taxation* was never printed but still exists in MS." [manuscript].

Happiness, Norman had discovered, could be achieved through a radical transformation in the way government funded the public's services. Society's problems lay not with how much was raised by taxation, but with how the money was raised. His formula would make the difference between misery and contentment, by "taking least from individuals and imposing the fewest sacrifices on them". He wanted "to show how the Revenue of a Country might be levied with least pressure on the Taxpayers". He confided in his Autobiography:

> "The conclusion to which I came was that a single Property Tax and that only was the scheme which offered the greatest advantages."

A single tax? Correctly applied, Norman's financial formula would free people to dissolve the economic and social problems which beset them. They could produce all the wealth and welfare they wanted. He anticipated the outcome:

---

1 D.P. O'Brien (2009), Introduction, *Taxation and the Promotion of Human Happiness*, Cheltenham: Edward Elgar, p.xvi-xvii.

"A great change in the public mind with respect to taxation would probably take place within a short period after the proposed scheme had come into operation. Almost every body would find that his income went farther than before, that he was practically richer...The well-being of the community would advance with accelerated speed, and direct imposts become less unpopular than now. Immediate advantage should be taken of this alteration in the popular voice, by increasing the property tax as fast as circumstances might allow, and lessening or altogether abolishing the indirect taxes that might still remain; and when all the latter had been thus commuted, the direct imposts, with the exception of the land tax might also be removed, leaving the latter and the property tax to supply all the wants of the Government."[2]

The happiness of the nation rested on the fate of one stream of income: the rent of land. But by laying bare the way in which rent was formed and distributed, Norman found to his horror that he was exposing the power base of the financial and cultural elites. How would those elites react, if he were to disclose the way in which Britain could scrap all the bad taxes and rely exclusively on rent to fund the State's services?

The financial algorithm

At the young age of 27 George Warde Norman was appointed a Director of the Bank of England. Ill-health alone prevented him from becoming the Governor. But he remained at the heart of the nation's financial affairs for half a century. Throughout this time, he was a prolific author of articles for the popular Press. He contributed to the *Economist* and the *Spectator*. He helped to steer the fate of the nation by shaping the financial system of the greatest imperial power in history. Through the Political Economy Club, which he co-founded, and his articles in the journals, he had the power to elevate the public discourse on economics.

Most importantly, he supported his theory on the way taxation affected the condition of the nation with first-hand experience. He had begun his working career as an entrepreneur, representing his father's timber importing business in Norway. And he observed at close quarters – while living in Hastings, on the Kent coast – how people were motivated to avoid taxes by engaging in smuggling.

As we shall see in Chapter 3, the tentacles of the Norman family reached into the 20th century with fatal consequences. It was not until the early years of the 21st century that *Taxation and the Promotion of Human Happiness* was finally published after a researcher stumbled on the manuscript in the archives of a public library in Kent.

Can we excuse Norman for his betrayal of the political science of governance? He wrote in his manuscript that, to overcome the resistance from people who did not have his depth of knowledge, "The government ought then in the first place to take every possible means of enlightening the public mind". Did he not have a

---

2 George Warde Norman (2009), *Taxation and the Promotion of Human Happiness*, edited by D.P. O'Brien with John Creedy, Cheltenham: Edward Elgar, p.195. Emphasis added.

moral obligation to contribute to that education?

The closest he came to divulging his secret was in 1850. His revelations appeared in a single paragraph buried deep in a pamphlet. His readers would have missed the significance of his world-changing insights, because he presented them as mere suggestions, "without an attempt to solve them, because their discussion would carry us too far, while at the same time, it is expedient to avoid the suspicion that they have been passed by unadvisedly".[3] In that one paragraph, he sought to salve his conscience. In failing to display the courage of his convictions, was he being cowardly? He presumed to instruct people on the myths they harboured about the taxes they paid. In his view, the time had come to spell out the facts. But his treatment of the subject was so elliptical that only those "in the know" could have decoded his message.

Norman offered three statements. When combined and correctly understood, he was alluding to a financial revolution.

First, on the nature of taxation. He referred to tithes, which were payments to support the church and clergy. But was a tithe a tax? Norman explained that it was not. He called it a "tithe rent-charge", because the revenue was drawn from the stream of rents. This is how he put it:

> "They are rather a portion of rent, appropriated to one party, the tithe owner, while the remaining portion of rent is appropriated to another party, the proprietor of the soil."

From this, Norman elucidated the ATCOR principle: all taxes come out of the rent. This principle of public finance was originally identified by the English political philosopher John Locke in the 17th century, and further analysed by Scottish moral philosopher Adam Smith in the 18th century.[4] But it was not until the early 19th century that the theory could be fully explored. Its implications relied on a rigorous analysis of the theory of rent. This was provided by David Ricardo (1772-1823), who had made his fortune as a stock broker. He elucidated the nature of taxes by considering their impact on the use of land. Rent, he stressed, was the measure of the taxable capacity of an economy.

In *Principles of Political Economy and Taxation*, Ricardo began with this crucial insight:

> "[I]t is quite certain, that a tax on the real rent of land falls wholly on the landlord... [I]t is from the net income of a country that all taxes are ultimately paid...A land-tax, levied in proportion to the rent of land, and varying with every variation of rent, is in effect a tax on rent..."[5]

Ricardo expounded his insights at the Political Economy Club, with Norman listening intently. He soon realised that Ricardo had omitted the "moral effects"

---

3 George Warde Norman (1850), *An Examination of some Prevailing Opinions, as to the Pressure of Taxation*, London: T. & W. Boone, p.52.

4 Fred Harrison, *The Traumatised Society* (2012), London: Shepheard-Walwyn, pp.183-187.

5 David Ricardo (1817), *Principles of Political Economy and Taxation*; in J.R. McCulloch, *The Works of David Ricardo*, London: John Murray, 1888, pp. 102, 105, 107.

from his theory. Norman began to explore the implications of the theory of rent. What, for example, would happen if a tax was abolished? He illustrated the process in terms of the tithe.

> "The abolition of tithe would deprive the tithe-owner of his share, and throw it entirely into the hands of the proprietor of the soil, in the form of increased rent."

If a tenant farmer was legally freed of the obligation to pay tithe, the money would not remain in his pocket. Under the fiscal policies employed by Parliament, the landlord was free to exercise his power to raise his rent by a corresponding sum. Norman recounted other examples of the ATCOR process. He discussed

▶ what would happen if the malt tax consumed by peasants was cut: "Its whole amount would…have been transferred to the landowner in the shape of rent";

▶ the toll-free transportation of manure: "Another instance of the influence of the landed interest in the legislature…its only effect being to raise rents"; and

▶ a tax on land transactions: "[The buyer] considers what the Land will cost him in tax and price altogether. The more he is obliged to pay in the way of tax, the less he will be disposed to give in the price".

The land market operated like a sponge. It soaked up the net income produced in the economy – that is, all the income that remained after deducting the wages of labour and the profits of capital, and which was not collected by government.

Norman's second insight concerned the impact on labour and capital, and on the price of goods and services traded in the markets. This is how he illustrated the economic impact of the tithe rent-charge on wages:

> "Tithe it is clear cannot constitute any burden upon the consumer, inasmuch as it does not affect price. The same principle is applicable to the land tax, and to the largest portion of the poor rate. Indeed it may be applied to all imposts on real property…or land tax, which constitutes so important an item in all Continental Budgets."

To an informed economist, this statement signalled a crucial insight. Public charges on rent were neutral: they did not affect prices in the markets. Nor did they influence people's behaviour. A public charge on rent did not distort either the allocation of productive resources or the consumption of goods and services. This was not the case with conventional taxes, which raised the costs of hiring labour, of employing capital and of consuming the products purchased in the market.

Norman's third point was the moral clincher. He starts by pointing out that the abolition of a tithe rent-charge would be unfair, because it "would be to give to the proprietor an additional benefit, for which he has never paid the price, and to which he has therefore no equitable claim". He then concludes the paragraph with this sentence:

"It may however be remarked, that a Government which possesses a large income in the character of co-proprietor with the possessors of the soil, ought to be in a condition to dispense with taxation to a proportionate extent."

The implications of these observations were explosive. Taxes could be abolished *in lieu* of rents. And if there was sufficient rent to cover all the costs of the State's expenditures, government could abolish all of the taxes that drove up prices and distorted the allocation and use of productive resources. In other words, government could fulfil its obligations with a Single Tax without damaging the production and distribution of income.

Norman was aware that, once upon a time, the English State had, indeed, relied almost exclusively on rent. One of his contemporaries was Richard Cobden, a member of the House of Commons and champion of free trade. In 1842, Cobden documented how the fiscal system had been corrupted over the previous 900 years. Up to the time of Henry VIII, the State was largely funded out of land rents (see graph). Then, as the State's rents were siphoned off by their lordships, and the tax burden was shifted onto the shoulders of landless peasants, Parliament found that it could not cover the costs of public services. So, government had to borrow to cover the deficit: sovereign indebtedness became an art of monetary manipulation to mask the failures of governance.

Norman could have employed his knowledge to powerful effect, given his association with the political and financial elites in London. By publicising the economics of the Single Tax, people would at least have had a standard against which to measure the performance of government. But he was too embedded in the culture of cheating. He could not bring himself to proclaim the financial

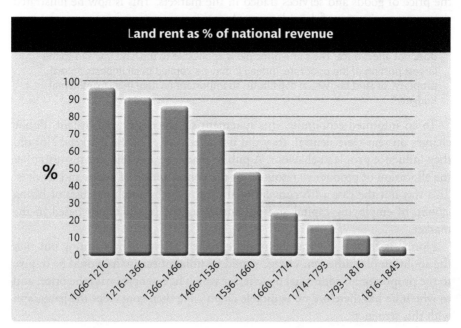

Land rent as % of national revenue

principles that he acknowledged as the cornerstone of a programme that would enhance the happiness of the nation.

The ladder to prosperity

By his silence, Norman helped to preserve the tax regime which automatically imposed the permanent condition of austerity on the social outcasts. By not employing the natural way of funding its services, governments are not able to balance their books. Consequently, they engage in deficit spending; and then, to try and restore order to the public's finances, they engage in debt reduction. This means that public services have to be reduced, either in quantity or quality.

What would happen if government reformed its revenue system according to Norman's happiness algorithm?

▶ Because of the ATCOR mechanism, tax cuts pay for themselves.

▶ Public services continue to be fully funded. Cuts in taxes on wages or profits are replaced by revenue from rent. The net gain is not soaked up by land owners.

▶ The population is not forced to endure austerity as the *quid pro quo* for reductions in taxes. We shall see in detail in Part III how everyone becomes richer.

▶ The rent-based system reduces the losses in wealth and welfare.

▶ Productivity of the population is increased. The net gains are shared as higher living standards for everyone.

▶ Increased revenue makes it possible for government to improve the quality of the services that people want.

By honouring the happiness principle, the creative freedom of people is enhanced to serve the bests interests of both the individual and society. But this is not how people are taught to perceive their best interests. Instead, they are persuaded to believe that they should do everything possible to "get on the housing ladder". The rent-seeking culture sponsors the myth that a rise in the price of houses means that there has been an increase in the wealth of the nation. This false proposition has been exposed by the chief economic commentator of the *Financial Times*.

Martin Wolf is a beneficiary of the way the rules governing the land market *redistributes* the wealth that is created by others. He is sitting on a £1m fortune, his share of the capital gain from what he calls the housing "racket".[6]

> "I own a house whose nominal value is perhaps 25 times as great as when I bought it 30 years ago, almost 9 times higher after adjusting for inflation. This vast increase in wealth is not due to my endeavours. It is overwhelmingly the product of a rise in the value of land, which is the fruit of other people's efforts, not mine."[7]

6 Martin Wolf, "Why we must halt the land cycle", *Financial Times*, July 8, 2010.
7 Martin Wolf, "Britain's self-perpetuating property racket", *Financial Times*, January 9, 2015.

Wolf's good fortune is more than offset by the pain endured by those who have to buy their shelter on terms dictated by the tax regime. He explains that land values, when traded, are no more than the transfer of income generated by others to those who own parcels of land. In their status as owners, people do not contribute to the production of that value. This redistribution is the result of "a corrupt arrangement whose result is to benefit the haves at the expense of the have-nots". The solution to this injustice, Wolf repeatedly affirmed in articles in the *Financial Times*, is the introduction of a public charge on the rent of land. But, he has pessimistically concluded, such an outcome is unlikely. It would be opposed by the vested interests. Today, those influential interests are not the landed aristocracy; they are the middle-class homeowners. The zeitgeist favours those who monopolise the nations socially created rents. This is one of the consequences of the acts and omissions of people like George Warde Norman.

Steps towards the Single Tax

In *Taxation and the Promotion of Human Happiness*, Norman spelt out the first step in the transition to an ethics-based finance:

"The system consists in the abolition of all the taxes now in operation, and their replacement by one general impost on property, which should take from each person possessing wealth in the community, an equal proportion of that wealth."

He makes it abundantly clear that the impost had to be on a single source of revenue: the rents that measured the value of the services provided by nature and by society. He followed up his pronouncement with this assurance: "Let not the imagination of the reader be terrified with the picture here portrayed to him". But in his public statements, Norman did not adopt that reassuring tone. In an article about Ireland which was published in *The Economist* (on February 22, 1868), he sounded this ominous warning: "It may be added that rents would never be paid to the States unless levied by force of arms".[8] If this were really to be the case, we may have some sympathy with Norman, who feared that his financial theorem would lead to "commotion and civil war". And yet, *not a single bullet was fired when the land tax was introduced in Denmark early in the 20th century.*[9] Norman applauded the progressive social policies applied in Denmark in the 19th century, which included a land-to-the-tiller law. Those policies laid the foundations for tax reform in the 20th century. It is no coincidence that Denmark is now classed as the No. 1 happiest nation on earth.[10]

But in the end, George Warde Norman's overriding concern was not for the people of Britain, but for the landlords whom he championed in an article

---

8 George Warde Norman (1869), *Papers on Various Subjects*, London: T. & W. Boone.
9 Ole Lefmann and Karsten K. Larsen (2000), "Denmark", in R.V. Andelson, *Land Value Taxation Around the World*, 3rd edn., Oxford: Blackwells.
10 *World Happiness Report* 2013, eds: John Helliwell et al., New York: Sustainable Development Solutions Network. The historical conditions that nurtured fiscal reform in Denmark are summarised in *The Bullet*, a video that may be accessed on https://www.youtube.com/user/geophilos

in *The Economist*. He wrote:

> "In conclusion, a few words may be said in defence of that much abused class – the landowners. They are neither much better nor much worse than other people. Like them they follow what they consider their own interests, but living as they do in glass houses peculiarly open to attack, they can hardly be exceptionally bad, and they certainly bear their full share of public burdens."[11]

The facts that exposed the lies in that *apologia* were concealed in his secret manuscript. Norman now renders us a service, in providing a case study of what can be achieved by the statecraft that commands the means to control the way people think and act. As for Norman's belief that, by remaining silent, this would save Britain from "Commotions and civil war", that was also a delusion. The people are locked into a perpetual civil war fought on the terrain of deprivation. A struggle between the Haves and Have-nots which remains unresolved to this day.

James E. Thorold Rogers (1823–1890)

Rent is the pre-eminent indicator of the health and wealth of the nation. Through the movement of prices in the land market, rent registers the dramas that are played out in the economy, as well as monitoring social and ecological trends. Rent is the sum of those events because it is the composite of the services of both nature and society. We can, therefore, "read" the state of humanity by carefully assessing the way in which rent is being formed and distributed. But that methodology is a threat to those who subjugate rent in order to preserve their privileged status. That was why discussion of the social role of rent was taboo in the 19th century. Norman's fears were not baseless. Cheating as a social process survives by messing with people's minds.

Censorship works at two levels. Self-censorship, for the sake of the easy life, was the course chosen by Norman. Free spirits, however, have to be contained by the institutions that are the props of the current regime, as one professor of economics at the University of Oxford discovered to his cost.

J.E. Thorold Rogers was elected Drummond Professor of Political Economy in 1862. As a student of history, he discovered that "One of the ways in which the owners of land have striven to maintain artificial rents has been, first, by

---

11 George Warde Norman (1868), "On the Ownership and Occupation of Land in England", *The Economist*, June 27.

starving the peasant, next by putting the cost of his necessary maintenance on other people".[12]

Rogers had somehow escaped the brainwashing. He was not someone who pulled his punches. So when he analysed the formation of rent, he did not compromise his language:

"The rents of the 17th century...began with competition rents which rapidly slid into famine rents, by which I mean rents which leave the occupiers with a bare maintenance, without the power of either improving or saving."

It was *Six Centuries of Work and Wages* that got him into trouble. He pointed the accusing finger as he traced the way the living conditions of the people of England were degraded over the centuries. The *productivity* of the nation had steadily increased. Under a justice-based revenue system, the working population in the 19th century ought to have been three or four times better off than their ancestors in the 16th century. Instead, they were worse off. This contradicted the authorised discourse which maintained that, providing people worked hard, they would improve their lot. Social progress was sold as an article of faith. Rogers provided the statistics to demonstrate the disconnect between doctrine and reality.

"I contend that, from 1563 to 1824, a conspiracy, concocted by the law and carried out by parties interested in its success, was entered into to cheat the English workman of his wages, to tie him to the soil, to deprive him of hope and to degrade him into irremediable poverty...For more than two centuries and a half the English law and those who administered the law were engaged in grinding the English workman down to the lowest pittance, in stamping out every expression or act which indicated any organised discontent, and in multiplying penalties upon him when he thought of his natural rights."[13]

Rogers had to be silenced. When he stood for re-election to his professorship (his term expired in 1867), his opponents nominated one Bonamy Price to oppose him. This was a gentleman "who had until recently been off his head", although the *Dictionary of National Biography* claimed that by the time of the election he had completely recovered his mental composure. Price won the election. Rogers was driven to earning his living by lecturing at a coaching establishment in the backwaters of London's Bayswater.

12 James E. Thorold Rogers (1891), *The Economic Interpretation of History*, 5th edn., London: T. Fisher Unwin, p.181.
13 James E. Thorold Rogers, MP (1903), *Six Centuries of Work and Wages*, 6th ed., London: Swan Sonnenschein, p.398.

2

Survival of the Unfit

ALL was not lost. George Warde Norman betrayed classical economics, but the happiness of the people of Britain might be secured by an alternative route. The French Revolution's legacy was a Europe in urgent need of a science of society. Auguste Comte articulated the principles of what he called sociology. His philosophical approach was that of the Parisian intellectual. Sociology needed a dose of Anglo empiricism. That came from the pen of a young journalist.

Herbert Spencer (1820-1903) was a critic who made his mark with 10 essays which he published in the *Nonconformist* in 1842 and 1843. In these, he set out the case against the Corn Laws. He favoured free trade, which would cut the cost of food. The landlords in Parliament, however, favoured protectionism, because it raised the rents of their farmland. And that, for Spencer, was a violation of natural law. The anti-Corn Law campaign inspired the creation of *The Economist*, which Spencer joined as a sub-editor in 1848. At about this time he began to write *Social Statics: The Conditions Essential to Human Happiness Specified, and the First of Them developed*. The book was published in 1850. It was a foundation text for the science of society.

Comte's approach was disappointing for Spencer, because it failed to clarify the reason why the inequality of incomes persisted in industrial society. That inequality yielded "a pathological state of unrest and social crisis".[1] Comte placed his faith in moral regulation aided by rational systems of religion and education. He knew something was wrong in society, but he could not identify the cause. He presumed that society, as a self-regulating organism, could integrate its constituent parts. To aid the understanding of how this happened, he formulated two branches of the new science.

▶ Social statics focused on the structure and function of institutions, whose interdependence was explained by the laws of co-existence.

---

1 James Fulcher and John Scott (2007), *Sociology*, 3rd edn., Oxford: Oxford University Press, p.27.

▶ Social dynamics explored how institutions changed over time. Sociologists would offer explanations for those changes.

But Comte could not come to terms with the brutal reality: Europe was hostage to a statecraft of greed. The proletarian revolution had guillotined the heads off the aristocracy and proclaimed equality, but it had failed to erase the patrician's culture of rent-seeking. Empiricism from across the channel provided the missing pieces.

Social Statics subjected Victorian society to forensic scrutiny. Spencer applied the concept of evolution to society before Charles Darwin applied it to nature. He did not share Comte's fatalistic view about the gross inequality that divided European societies. Scientists could propose remedies. His brilliant achievement appeared as Chapter 9 of *Social Statics*. What he called *The Right to the Use of the Earth* was a trenchant critique of the way in which socially-generated income had been privatised. The rules of tenure converted most people into trespassers in the land of their birth. This turned property laws into "an infringement of the law of equal freedom".[2]

Spencer denied "the rectitude of property in land". No passage of time or number of transactions could legitimise the injustice that stemmed from the original land grab. Title deeds, ultimately, were based on fraud. Land was a bequest from God, and society was the steward of people's individual right of access to earth. Spencer was uncompromising.

"In our tender regard for the vested interests of the few, let us not forget that the rights of the many are in abeyance, and must remain so, as long as the earth is monopolised by individuals. Let us remember, too, that the injustice thus inflicted on the mass of mankind is an injustice of the gravest nature."[3]

The political implications were clear, for "if pushed to its ultimate consequences a claim to exclusive possession of the soil involves a landowning despotism".

In Spencer's view, the highest civilisation would be based on a form of tenure in which people were co-heirs of the soil. Owners should pay rent to society in exchange for the benefits they received from occupation of land. By this means, "the earth might be enclosed, occupied, and cultivated in entire subordination to the law of equal freedom".

Spencer's analysis proved the value of sociology as a discipline that could stand alongside classical economics. He invoked the moral case for removing the injustice that blighted the nation. His practical conclusions harmonised with the policies advocated by Adam Smith. Together, economics and sociology could advance society along an evolutionary trajectory grounded in the principles of both fairness and efficiency. At the heart of their model of society was the rectitude of a public finance that socialised the nation's rents and privatised the earnings of people's labour.

---

2 Herbert Spencer (1850), *Social Statics*; New York: Robert Schalkenbach Foundation, 1995, p. 104.
3 Spencer (1850: 112).

Spencer was emphatic: "[T]o deprive others of their rights to the use of the earth is to commit a crime inferior only in wickedness to the crime of taking away their lives or personal liberties".[4] That insight resonated with people whose ancestors had been expelled from their traditional habitats. Enclosure of the English commons continued into the 19th century, so Spencer was not dealing with a fossilised practise. His analysis was a direct challenge to the survival of the aristocracy as the landed elite. His chorus on liberty could not be left on the public record. It had to be expunged from the public's consciousness. There was one way only for the words to be deleted: the author had to be bought off.

Sell-out Spencer

In the annals of scientific thought, there are few betrayals to compare with Herbert Spencer's heinous rejection of his own work.

People are entitled to change their minds if they discover errors in the evidence. In Spencer's case, the facts did not change. He did.

As a philosopher of the theory of evolution he coined the phrase "survival of the fittest", which Darwin adopted.[5] As his fame spread, his celebrity status attracted invitations to the fashionable salons in London and speaking tours in America. He acquired a taste for the sporting life, a preoccupation in which he could indulge as weekend guest at the stately homes of the aristocracy. Herbert Spencer was seduced by the good life. And so, he modified his views about the right of land owners to pocket the nation's rents. When *Social Statics* was republished in 1892, Chapter 9 was missing. "I had relinquished some of the conclusions drawn from the first principles laid down," he declared in the Preface to the new edition. Gone was all mention of the evils he had originally associated with land monopoly.

In the intervening 40 years, he churned out a veritable library of books on biology, ethics and philosophy. Through them we can trace how he contorted his mind to accommodate the rejection of his original analysis of land tenure. Hypocrisy now infused his definition of justice. Justice required that there

"shall be maintained a due proportion between returns and labours: the natural relation between work and welfare shall be preserved intact. Justice [entailed the] principle of equivalence which meets us when we seek its roots in the laws of individual life."[6]

According to this formulation, landlords *failed the test of equivalence between returns and labour, between work and welfare*. Landlords appropriated a share of their tenants' labours without contributing anything to the process of production. They were entitled to a return on the capital equipment which they may have provided for their tenants, but that income was not "rent". Call it profit, or

---

4 Spencer (1850: 112).
5 Charles Darwin (1868), *The Variation of Animals and Plants under Domestication*, London: Murray, p.17.
6 Herbert Spencer (1879), *The Principles of Ethics*; 1978, Indianapolis: Liberty Fund, Vol. 1, p.312.

interest, or anything you like; it was in a different category to *economic rent*.

The social implication of Spencer's sell-out may be gauged by considering the failure of British statecraft to erase what he called (in Chapter 2 of *Social Statics*) "The Evanescence of Evil". Such evil was not just physical pain. His examples of "moral evil" are listed in Box 2.1. They stemmed from a single cause – "want of congruity between the faculties and their spheres of action".

Box 2.1 **Manifestations of "moral evil"**	
Spencer's examples	**Problems persisting into the 21st century**
Distress at the sight of misery	In 2015 nearly half of jobless young people were too depressed to even leave their homes, their plight causing misery to parents.[1]
Unhappy bachelor who cannot afford to marry	3.7m young adults will still be living with parents in 2020, an increase of 700,000 since 2013. According to the Office of National Statistics, housing costs force an increased number of families to cohabit, contributing to decline in marriages.[2]
Mother mourning her lost child	Data for births in 2013 show that mortality rates are highest among babies born in areas of poverty.[3]
The emigrant who laments his fatherland	Migration remains the only solution for many searching for work. The Irish case is documented in Chapter 5.
Unemployment	Involuntary unemployment on a systemically significant scale is a permanent feature of the economy.
Lifetime spent in a distasteful occupation	Career counselling remains incapable of helping people into jobs "in harmony with the nature of the man".[4]

Sources
1 Prince's Trust Macquarie Youth Index 2015 http://www.princes-trust.org.uk/pdf/Youth_Index_2015_Report.PDF
2 National Housing Federation (2013), *Housing Britain's Future*, London, p.5. Emily Cadman (2015), "Rising property prices swell number of households containing two or more families", *Financial Times*, January 29.
3 Bradley N. Manktelow et al. (2015), *Perinatal Mortality Surveillance Report* (June), MBRRACE-UK.
4 W. Norton Grubb (2002), *An Occupation in Harmony*, Paris: OECD, p.21.

Conveniently for Spencer, his version of the theory of evolution ensured that "evil perpetually tends to disappear". People adapt themselves to their environments. Adaptation was to be observed in "the acclimatization of plants, in the altered habits of domesticated animals, in the varying characteristics of our own race". And yet, the "moral evils" which he listed continue to haunt humanity. Those evils are not random; nor are they unrelated. They remain the product of a cult-like process which stubbornly prevents millions of people from achieving what Spencer called happiness. His definition of that state points us in the direction of the force that underpinned his moral evils:

"Happiness signifies a gratified state of all the faculties. The gratification of a faculty is produced by its exercise. To be agreeable, that exercise must be proportionate to the power of the faculty; if it is insufficient, discontent arises, and its excess produces weariness."

According to *Social Statics*, there was just one explanation for the inability of people to achieve their potential: they were prevented from working in ways that gratified them into the state of happiness. All the examples of his forms of evil can be traced back to the privatisation of socially created rent. But sociology was not going to serve as a tool for erasing that evil, because Spencer disabled the discipline.

As he relished his new way of life as a celebrity, Spencer abandoned his "law of equal freedom", which he had defined thus:

"We have seen that the right of property is deducible from the law of equal freedom, that it is presupposed by the human constitution, and that its denial involves absurdities."

By eviscerating people's equal right of access to their natural environments, Spencer undermined his claim to be applying the scientific method. He exposed himself as a charlatan. In bringing down the blinkers on the minds of future generations of students (Box 2.2), he helped to perpetuate the evils that would cause misery on an unparalleled scale in the 20th century.

Box 2.2 **How minds are censured**
Herbert Spencer's influence on the science of society may be gauged by assessing the contents of a teaching manual published by Oxford University Press. The volume was selected at random to review its treatment of the classical factors of production (land, labour and capital). In a textbook of more than 900 pages that is used to instruct students on how laws and institutions shape social behaviour, land did not rate a single reference in the index. Students are taught a caricature of the science of society.

Textbook treatment of economic categories: number of references	
Labour (government/market/movement/parties	50
Capital (ism/ist/class/society)	50
Land (lords/rent/monopoly)	0

Source: James Fulcher and John Scott (2007), *Sociology*, 3rd edn., Oxford: Oxford University Press.

To rationalise his betrayal, Spencer had to redefine his theory of property. He provided his new account in an Appendix to *The Principles of Ethics*. If the genesis of land ownership entailed iniquities, he wrote, these were committed by the ancestors "of all existing men".[7] Guilt should be shared even by landless peasants!

---

7 Herbert Spencer (1893), *The Principles of Ethics*; Indianapolis: Liberty Fund, 1978, Vol. 2, p.455.

And if that was not sufficient to silence the critics of landlords, he pointed out that, while those critics lamented the injustice in their home territory, they were silent about the land grabbing that was taking place abroad. The critics were hypocrites!

Spencer's clinching argument in favour of the status quo relied on a false account of the alternative. Nationalisation of land, he argued, would result in worse evils.

> "Under the existing system of ownership, those who manage the land, experience a direct connection between effort and benefit; while, were it under state ownership, those who managed it would experience no such direct connection. The vices of officialism would inevitably entail immense evils."[8]

But nationalisation was not the only option, and Spencer knew it. An alternative strategy had been propounded by an American journalist, and Spencer knew that it did not involve taking anybody's land. Nor did it transfer the power of land to the State.

The voice from San Francisco

A book which addressed the issue of inequality was published in 1879. Henry George worked as a journalist in San Francisco. He had been puzzled by the poverty which co-existed with vast amounts of unused land in California. Why were so many people going hungry? His book echoed the analysis in Spencer's Chapter 9. *Progress and Poverty* became the first best-selling text on economics in history, and it inspired the first global reform movement.

Henry George approvingly cited *Social Statics*. Justice would be achieved if those who possessed land were obliged to pay for the benefits they received. The solution was a Land Tax. By the time Spencer read that book, he was embarrassed to be reminded of his original analysis. He noted, in a letter to the *St. James's Gazette*, that he had tried to read *Progress and Poverty* "which I closed after a few minutes on finding how visionary were its ideas".[9]

In fact, Henry George was more pragmatic than Spencer. Social Statics proposed that land should be taken into State ownership so that, instead of paying rent "to the agent of Sir John or his Grace, he would pay it to an agent or deputy agent of the community". This formula meant that "all men would be equally land-lords, all men would be alike free to become tenants", an arrangement in which "the earth might be enclosed, occupied and cultivated, in entire subordination to the law of equal freedom". Not necessary, argued Henry George. The alternative was simpler.

> "I do not propose either to purchase or to confiscate private property in land...Let the individuals who now hold it still retain, if they want to, possession of what they

---

8 *The Principles of Ethics*, p.460.
9 Cited in Henry George (1937), *A Perplexed Philosopher*, London: Henry George Foundation, p.57.

are pleased to call their land...Let them buy and sell, and bequeath and devise it...
It is not necessary to confiscate land; it is only necessary to confiscate rent."[10]

That word *confiscate* was unfortunate. It allowed the rent-seekers to scream *socialist* at George, who was as ardent an advocate of the free market as Adam Smith. George proposed a funding arrangement in which people would keep what they created (*ergo*, no taxes on earned incomes). Instead, they should pay for what they received. The net effect: rent would be paid into the public purse in return for enjoying the services provided by public agencies.

Henry George, as an outsider, was not able to influence the British Establishment in the way that (say) a Director of the Bank of England might have done. It was easier to ostracise him. But George persisted with his campaign for justice. The rent-seekers realised that the notion of a single source of revenue – the rents of the kingdom – was a direct threat to their something-for-nothing way of life. The tactics employed on Spencer – buying him off – would not work with George. An alternative strategy was needed.

The first moves took place in America. The Robber Barons were the New World's most successful rent-seekers. They could not secure immortality through the primogeniture that created landed dynasties in the Old World, but (disguising themselves as philanthropists) they could do so by endowing universities and professorships. The beneficiaries understood that there was a price to be paid for that generosity. The machinations of professors on both sides of the Atlantic have been meticulously documented by Mason Gaffney, emeritus professor of economics at the University of California.[11] The classical concept of rent disappeared from economics, driven below the statistical radar. Land was downgraded into a sub-species of capital. No distinction was acknowledged between (say) the power of a tractor and the fertility of land. Once again, the rent-seekers could sleep easily – and grow richer – in their beds.

Survival of the fittest?

By renouncing the formula that freedom is contingent on each person's right of equal access to the riches of nature, Herbert Spencer played his part in depriving people of their right of equal access to the riches of society. The cumulative effect was the psychological, spiritual and physical deprivation of society's outcasts. But Spencer's influence reached beyond the first-order victims of land monopolisation. He coloured the consciousness of those who were in the business of thinking about the human condition. This impact on the community of social philosophers of the late 19th century, to which contemporary ideologues like George Warde Norman contributed, was reviewed by Harvard historian Stuart Hughes in these terms:

---

10 Henry George (1879), *Progress and Poverty*; New York: Robert Schalkenbach Foundation, 1979, p.405.
11 Mason Gaffney (1994), "Neo-classical Economics as a Stratagem against Henry George", in Mason Gaffney and Fred Harrison, *The Corruption of Economics*, London: Shepheard-Walwyn.

"The 18th or early 19th century image of man as a self-consciously rational being freely selecting among properly weighed alternatives they dismissed as an anti-quated illusion. Some such conviction of the inevitable limitations on human freedom – whether by physical circumstance or through emotional condition – has become the unstated major premise of contemporary social science. Sociologists and anthropologists, economists and psychologists are at one in confining within narrow limits the realm of conscious choice."[12]

Those scholars, unwittingly, became one of the constraining influences on people's freedom to choose in the 20th century. But the impoverishment of humanity, as a direct result of the intellectual dishonesty of Herbert Spencer, was not confined to the debasement of social science. Biology was also victimised.

Charles Darwin's theory of evolution transformed people's perception of the origins of life on earth. Spencer's version reassured the ruling class that Might was Right. There could be no moral dilemmas, now, because class divisions reflected the natural order of things. Inequality was not the result of bad laws but of good biology. As a consequence, biology was also subordinated to the service of Spencer's mission to defend the *status quo*. His "survival of the fittest" reassured the owners of land that their wealth was the result of their superiority. This contributed to the social Darwinist view that some men were biologically inferior. That doctrine found its expression in the eugenics movement which evolved into Nazi racism.

The distortion of the analytical tools of biology resulted in the waste of a huge amount of brain power. Biologists had to devote the best part of a century to unravelling the linguistic knots caused by Spencer's use of the word "fittest". Social scientists who might otherwise have attended to the root causes of deprivation also wasted their time and effort. Diane Paul notes how

"evolution through the 'survival of the fittest' came readily to imply the dependence of progress on laissez-faire economics. It came also to imply the need for social policies aimed at increasing the birth rate of the more prosperous classes."[13]

Longevity, if that is how "survival" is measured, does not necessarily prove the fitness of genes or culture to prevail. If our concern is with the evolution of humanity, fitness must first and foremost be related to the cultural DNA which best serves the common good. The qualities of the commons determine the capacity of each generation to achieve its wellbeing. But collective wellbeing cannot be optimised if we deprive any individual of the equal right to try and realise his or her potential. That right is denied if society fails to tailor its rules in ways that lead to the fulfilment of what the classical philosophers called happiness. The sum total of happiness remains far below what could be achieved. This bears witness to the survival of doctrines that are unfit to rule.

Today, we continue to grapple with the mean spirit infused into the discourses on governance by Herbert Spencer. He presented his doctrine of welfare benefits

---

12 H. Stuart Hughes (1967), *Consciousness and Society*, London: MacGibbon & Kee, p.4.
13 Diane B. Paul (1988), "The Selection of the 'Survival of the Fittest'", *J. of the History of Biology*, Vol.21(3).

in his discussion on whether the landless should be compensated for their loss. Well, declared Spencer, since 1601 the poor had received £500m in the form of Poor Law handouts. That was the contribution from the rent of land. If anything, he was assured by one land owner, this was an underestimate.[14] *The poor had been paid off!* The conclusion was inevitable: "individual ownership, subject to state suzerainty, should be maintained".

Boris Johnson (1964-)

If those who govern conform to codes of conduct that are unfit for purpose, *how do they sustain their misgovernance through the generations?* To retain control, their culture must be adept at recruiting new foot soldiers.

In the 20th century, Margaret Thatcher was the archetype foot soldier. As Britain's Prime Minister, she ridiculed sociology as a discipline. Herbert Spencer's influence may be detected in Thatcher's famous proclamation (in an interview in *Women's Own* in 1987): "There's no such thing as society: there are individual men and women, and there are families". With the aid of such doctrines, the political Right managed to concentrate attention on the individual and *laissez-faire*, giving a free run to the rent-seeking culture. Thatcher's legacies are pure rent-seeking.

▶ *Abolition of the property tax.* Thatcher wanted to eliminate the tax tailored to the value of the public services. Owners of high-value properties would be the winners. The revenue burden would be transferred to low-income families as a flat-rate tax on each person's head. The exercise was defeated by popular opposition in 1990.

▶ *Sale of council houses.* Under the guise of advancing a "property-owning democracy", Thatcher initiated the sale of social housing to tenants at subsidised prices. Low-income families would be given a taste of the fruits of land ownership. Many of them cashed in, selling their homes to pocket the capital gains.

Thatcher's mantle was picked up in the 21st century by a new recruit: Boris Johnson, the Mayor of London who was elected back into Parliament in 2015 as the Member for the Conservative safe seat of Uxbridge and South Ruislip.

---

14 *The Principles of Ethics*, p.459.

His schooling had prepared him as a foot soldier for the creed that "greed is good". He was educated at Eton and Balliol College, Oxford. His ambition was to become leader of the Conservative Party; and, thereafter, the Prime Minister of Great Britain. A humorous demeanour and dishevelled appearance disarmed his opponents as he insisted that it was "futile" to try and end inequality. Genetics supported his politics.

> "Whatever you may think of the value of IQ tests, it is surely relevant to a conversation about equality that as many as 16 per cent of our species have an IQ below 85, while about 2 per cent have [sic] an IQ above 130. The harder you shake the pack, the easier it will be for some cornflakes to get to the top...I stress – I don't believe that economic equality is possible; indeed some measure of inequality is essential for the spirit of envy and keeping up with the Joneses that is, like greed, a valuable spur to economic activity."[15]

Thatcher had put the Great back into Britain, he reminded his audience.

> "Of the 193 present members of the UN, we have conquered or at least invaded 171 – that is 90 per cent. The only countries that seem to have escaped were places like Andorra and the Vatican City. In the period 1750 to 1865 we were by far the most politically and economically powerful country on earth."[16]

This was straight out of Herbert Spencer's doctrine of the survival of the fittest. Greed, insisted the Mayor, was a "valid motivator...for economic progress". The rich should be applauded for their contribution to the costs of public services. The top 1% of earners contributed 30% of income tax.

> "That is an awful lot of schools and roads and hospitals that are being paid for by the super-rich. So why, I asked innocently, are they so despicable in the eyes of all right-thinking people?"

I provided the answer to Johnson's question in *Ricardo's Law*. Thanks to the way politicians like Johnson had rigged the public's finances, rich people claw back more than their lifetime's taxes through the housing market. Total fiscal payments are more than offset by the capital gains which they reap from their residential properties. That alchemy does not work for taxpaying tenants. In fact, they subsidise the public services enjoyed by the rich. But Johnson was not interested in dissecting the realities of the tax system. From his prime-time platforms, he broadcast the doctrines which perpetuate the culture of cheating. That may not have been his conscious intent, but it was the practical outcome.

Using Johnson's brand of analysis would not resolve society's problems. Where a person is located on the spectrum of Greed-to-Goodness, or by using metrics that compared Avarice *versus* Altruism, is irrelevant. What matters is how a person gets rich. By adding to the wealth of the nation? Or extracting other people's wealth? Johnson avoids that approach, which equips him to eulogise the existing

---

15 Boris Johnson (2013), Annual Margaret Thatcher Lecture, Centre for Policy Studies, London, November 27. http://www.cps.org.uk/events/q/date/2013/11/27/the-2013-margaret-thatcher-lecture-boris-johnson/
16 Fred Harrison (2006), *Ricardo's Law: House Prices and the Great Tax Clawback Scam*, London: Shepheard-Walwyn, pp. 21-24.

system. And anyway, as he triumphantly pointed out in 2013, his socialist adversaries had failed to propose a viable alternative social model.

> "What has been really striking about the last five or six years is that no one on the Left – no one from Paul Krugman to Joe Stiglitz to Will Hutton, let alone Ed Miliband – has come up with any other way for an economy to operate except by capitalism. We all waited for the paradigm shift, after the crash of 2008. The Left was ushered centre stage, and missed their cue; political history reached a turning point, and failed to turn. Almost a quarter of a century after the collapse of Soviet and European communism – a transformation that Mrs Thatcher did so much to bring about – there has been no intellectual revival of her foes...Like it or not, the free market economy is the only show in town."

Therein lay the philosophical crisis that afflicts Britain; and, indeed, the western world. The rent-seekers control the terms of debate and, therefore, the collective consciousness. Their culture defines the meaning of concepts like *capitalism* and *free market*. What was treated as no more than a banking crisis has come and gone, leaving the elites unscathed. With the honourable exception of Joseph Stiglitz, the Nobel laureate, no-one with open access to the mainstream media could coherently apply economic theory to make sense of the cheating in the financial sector. Which brings us to our next problem: what had turned money-men into rent-seekers?

3

"Not Cheating? Not Trying!"

THEY are Masters of the Universe. But the universe inhabited by bankers runs parallel to planet Earth. From it, they radiate their webs to ensnare the lives of mortals, a feat accomplished by wrapping a psychotic membrane around their prey in the way that a spider traps its quarry in a web before consuming it.

To sustain the psychotic narrative, I have to do two things.

1. *Demonstrate* that bankers have their fingers in the public purse on a scale that gives them a share of the power of the State; a power to control people by moulding culture to manipulate thoughts and behaviour.

By analysing the provenance of a nation's taxable income – the net product of the economy – we can trace how the financial sector systematically misappropriates a significant part of the nation's revenue.

2. *Prove* that financiers behave irresponsibly; driven by a quest for riches and with a mandate to behave in a rent-seeking manner that is not constrained by the moral codes that discipline the population.

By analysing the origins of High Finance, we can trace how the sovereign State ceded its authority over the nation's money to financiers. Political protection for that privileged status is, in turn, secured by a regulatory regime that camouflages the operations of those who get rich without adding value to the wealth of the nation.

Politicians and economists conspire with bankers to keep reality at arm's length. Whether they do so wittingly or through ignorance is beside the point. Their influence legitimises the dealings that are conducted with deception aforethought. This proposition will be tested by considering typical transactions in the housing market. But first, to de-construct the duplicity, we need to locate current activity in its cultural and historical context.

The systematic brutalisation of the peoples of Europe began in earnest in the 16th century. Monarchs and their courtiers triggered the process that deprived people of the traditional land rights that gave them their independent means of material support. The aim of the land grab was to privatise the feudal State's primary source of revenue: rents generated on the territory. To facilitate what was a financial coup against the State, land had to be monetised. Only then could rents be filtered through the market and into private pockets. This required the collaboration of money-lenders. In Britain, the nobility sought the aid of the goldsmiths who conducted their business in the City of London's coffee shops. Between them, the land-enclosing barons and the merchants who abetted them engineered a larceny unparalleled in criminal history.

Once their lordships had tasted the something-for-nothing Good Life, there was no stopping them. The destruction of villages and hamlets acquired its own momentum. Attempts were made to push back against this tide of change, but the fight to restore traditional rights proved to be hopeless. For with the passage of time, the nobility adapted the laws of the land and the sensibilities of the population to accommodate their mission.

Urgent adjustments were needed in the financial sector. The industrial mode of production was looming, which promised new riches as high-energy techniques made it possible to peel back more layers of nature's rents (such as those from coal and hydro power). Industrialisation required a monetary system that could achieve the twin aims of facilitating commerce, while channelling the increased rents to the rent-seekers. The English, the Irish, Scottish and Welsh were ready to perform a miracle. They had found new ways to fructify wealth through the mass production of goods. Britain was about to detach herself from the seasonal rhythms and material constraints imposed by nature. But this voyage of discovery into a post-agricultural age was conditional. The top slice of the increased wealth had to be reserved for a class which, in its status as the claimant of rent, would be excused from contributing to the added value. That was the law of the land. And the financiers consecrated that arrangement. But to pull off the deception, a new language was needed, one that could be used in the High Streets to deceive folk as they went about their daily business. Thus did the bankers tie themselves into a culture of irresponsibility. If the land owners were reaping rents without contributing value to the wealth of the nation, a corresponding system would need to emerge for the benefit of the financiers.

For a glimpse into the foundations of this part of the story, we can return to the period which was closely observed – and influenced – by George Warde Norman. Norman lived through the first three major financial crises of the industrial era. He called them "bubbles". As a director of the Bank of England, he was "a leader of the move to codify gold standard rules, which were embodied in the Bank Act of 1844".[1] The psychotic nature of that legislation – its disconnectedness from economic reality – was demonstrated by what happened when the crises struck.

Norman's first experience with a financial crisis was with the one that followed the war with France in 1825. He divided his time between fire-fighting the financial crisis at the Bank of England, and trying to reduce the losses to his

---

1 Liaquat Ahamed (2010), *Lords of Finance*, London: Windmill Books, p. 82.

timber business, and from his speculation in a Mexican mining operation. He also lost heavily in the 1837 crisis; losses mainly incurred through the stock he held in American companies. "I bore my losses with very tolerable equanimity. In truth, I was never very fond of money and knew that I had enough left for my wants," he noted in his *Autobiography*.

By the 1840s, Norman was equipped, both theoretically and based on his business experiences, to recommend remedial action to forestall further booms and busts. There is no ambiguity about his influence on the financial fate of Britain at this crucial point in history. With two others, he was "the architect of the intellectual framework" that underpinned the Bank Charter Act of 1844.[2] The Act was intended to reorganise the way the Bank of England conducted its business; especially by regulating the value of the notes it could issue. The Bank failed to manage the nation's money supply in a manner that might have fore-stalled the crisis of 1847. Norman wrote that he was "deeply mortified by the apparent failure of the Act". That failure was repeated with the booms that turned to busts in 1857 and 1866. In response to each of these three major crises, the Act was suspended.[3] What does that reveal about the competence of the lawmakers who were stewards of the nation's finances? In the upswing of the business cycle the legislation was not capable of delivering long-term stability. And then, when a crisis struck, the legislation obstructed the Bank of England's ability to intervene, and had to be suspended. Here was a manifestation of social psychosis in action!

Norman had diligently studied the theory of rent, so he was competent to explain to his fellow Directors at the Bank that the booms were driven by rent-seeking. Manipulating the interest rate would have little impact on the deci-sions in the land market which were driving the business cycle. But Norman's self-censorship prevented him from sharing that knowledge. Financial doctrines that were not anchored in the real world coloured the minds of law-makers and Directors at the Bank of England. This would give free rein to the causes of crises such as the one that struck Britain in 2008.

Thus was incubated the psychotic institutional and legal framework that presided over the nation's finances in the 20th century. The proposition that the organising principle of High Finance is psychotic may be illustrated by consider-ing two familiar episodes: one from the realm of political governance, the other from the realm of financial governance.

---

2 D.P. O'Brien and John Creedy (2010), *Darwin's Clever Neighbour*, Cheltenham: Edward Elgar, p.417, n.188.
3 Walter Bagehot (1915), *Lombard Street*, London: Smith, Elder, pp.193-194.

Hallucinations and Delusions: I

Gordon Brown spent 10 years as Britain's Chancellor of the Exchequer. Throughout this period he claimed that he was acting in the best interests of the population at large. To aid him, he had at his disposal all of the resources of HM Treasury.

He was acutely aware of the cyclical instability of the UK economy, and so he set out to build stability into the system. His favourite mantra (chanted in and out of Parliament) was the promise of "no more booms and busts". As chancellor, he could have reframed the fiscal system to favour those who added value; and tone down the incentives that privileged those who made money out of thin air. Following his tenure at the Treasury, he moved next door to No 10 Downing Street when Tony Blair resigned as Prime Minister. And so, it was as head of the government that Gordon Brown presided over the end of the property boom that went bust in 2008.

Was Brown an innocent victim, deluded by powers unseen? Were his words and deeds in HM Treasury driven by hallucination?

In 1997, when they came to power, I wrote personal letters to Prime Minister Tony Blair, Chancellor of the Exchequer Gordon Brown, and three of their closest associates in HM Treasury and Downing Street. I alerted them to the way in which increasing sums of money would pour up the property ladder until the house of cards collapsed as prices peaked in 2007 (the peak came in the fourth quarter of 2007). This would then be followed by a banking crisis and a depression.[4] The timing of these events could be deduced from the patterns of history.[5] A responsible form of governance, one that was anchored in the world of reality, in which legislators fulfilled their duty of care to the people, would have taken remedial action.

My letter to Gordon Brown was dated November 4, 1997. The reply was dated December 9, and it said:

"The Chancellor and his advisers are always happy to receive ideas and suggestions. I cannot comment on your points in detail, but I can assure you that your points have been noted and will be carefully considered for future budgets."

No appropriate action was taken in the nine budgets that preceded the peak in house prices. The financial crisis that struck the UK financial sector in 2008 was an avoidable event. Brown led Britain by the nose into that financial disaster. Mass unemployment and home repossessions were the outcome.

This history reveals the hallmarks of a psychotic state of affairs in the realms of Power Politics.

---

4 Fred Harrison (1997), *The Chaos Makers*, London: Vindex, p.27; (2010), *2010 The Inquest*, London, free download from www.sharetherents.org
5 Fred Harrison (1983), *The Power in the Land*; and (2005), *Boom Bust: House Prices, Banking and the Depression of 2010*, London: Shepheard-Walwyn.

Hallucinations and Delusions: II

Is High Finance wreathed in delusion and hallucination, detached from reality in a way that renders it irresponsible for what happens to people in the real world? If Mark Carney is to be believed, that would seem to be the case. On June 10, 2015, the Governor of the Bank of England declared an end to irresponsibility in the City of London. In a speech at Mansion House, he announced:

> "The age of irresponsibility is over. Though markets can be powerful drivers of prosperity, markets can go wrong. Left unattended, they are prone to instability, excess and abuse."

The terms of that re-assurance are delusional. The financial markets had not been "left unattended". Financiers in the City of London were regulated by laws and institutions sanctioned by Parliament. And the new layer of regulations that led Carney to pronounce the end of irresponsibility does not erase the culture that drives the cheating that is an embedded feature of the banking sector. The Bank of England and other regulatory agencies actively supervised the City of London in the years leading up to the seizure of the banks in 2008. Nobody in positions of power pressed the Red Alert button to warn the customers of banks that a meltdown was in the offing. The irresponsible behaviour of the regulators was acknowledged by Mervyn King, who was Governor of the Bank of England at the time. Reminiscing on BBC radio, he insisted that no one person or political party was to blame:

> "I am not going to talk about individual parties' culpability because I think the real problem was a shared intellectual view right across the entire political spectrum and shared across the financial markets that things were going pretty well. There were imbalances – we knew things were unsustainable – but it was not entirely obvious where it would come unstuck – and I think that is something everyone shared, and the right thing is to make it better for the future. Looking back the leverage of banks was absurdly high and should have been lower. I don't think there is any point blaming them for it. It came as an enormous surprise to everyone that banks were not creditworthy."

Despite the benefit of hindsight, King was not sure that politicians had "yet got to the heart of what went wrong".[6] Could it be that he, Mervyn King, was in part responsible for the confusion that compromised the minds of politicians (Box 3.1)?

This history reveals all the hallmarks of a psychotic state of affairs in the realms of High Finance.

---

6 Patrick Wintour (2014), "Labour not responsible for crash, says former Bank of England governor", *The Guardian*, December 29.

Box 3.1 **The Governor's blind spot**

Mervyn King and his co-author, John Kay, were professors of economics when they wrote their textbook on taxation. Kay believes that "Politicians cannot be trusted to set the fiscal rules".[1] Can economists be trusted?

King and Kay acknowledge, in a chapter devoted to "Taxing economic rent", that "rent could be taxed, or otherwise reduced, without any economic distortion resulting". But while noting that "the underlying intellectual argument for seeking to tax economic rent retains its force", they added the killer claim: "[I]t is apparent that the total of economic rents, of all kinds, is not now a sufficiently large proportion of national income for this to be a practicable means of obtaining the resources needed to finance a modern State".[2]

This pronouncement is not grounded in reality. It is a favourite shibboleth of post-classical economists that survives because of incompetence and the refusal to interrogate the facts. For a prime example, see the case of Paul Krugman (below, p.100).

1 John Kay (2008), "Politicians cannot be trusted to set the fiscal rules", *Financial Times*, September 2.
2 Mervyn King and John Kay (1990), *The British Tax System*, 5th ed., Oxford: Oxford University Press, pp.178-179.

Do you bank on money?

The art of inducing the state of psychosis is illustrated by the way in which the rent-seeking culture wraps layers of fiction around people's minds. The language of deception is standard practice in High Finance. The evidence is displayed in the information racks on the walls of every bank on the high streets of Britain.

Bankers want us to believe that they are engaged in the production of wealth. They do so by providing a service which includes "lending" money to their customers. Their "products" are "deposited" in customers' bank accounts. That deposit comes at a price: the "interest" payable on the "loans" of their "money".

It's all a fabrication. A Big Lie.

Banks do not have vaults stashed with cash waiting to be loaned to "borrowers". You do *not* "borrow" money from a bank to buy a house. But the myth persists, endorsed by the authority of the Bank of England.

"Commercial banks create money, in the form of bank deposits, by making new loans. When a bank makes a loan, for example to someone taking out a mortgage to buy a house, it does not typically do so by giving them thousands of pounds worth of banknotes. Instead, it credits their bank account with a bank deposit of the size of the mortgage. **At that moment, new money is created.**"[7]

The Bank of England is assumed to be the authority on money. It affirms that High Street banks make "loans" and that in doing so they create new money. This is a false account of what actually happens, but it is treated as the gospel truth. So where does money really come from?

You create it.

We all create it, as we go about our daily business.

7 Michael McLeay et al. (2014), *Money in the Modern Economy*, Bank of England Quarterly Bulletin, Q1, p.3.

Our concern here is with the credit that is part of the "money supply" which is not conjured from thin air, but is anchored in the real world. It is created by working people. How this is accomplished emerges as we work our way through a typical transaction: the purchase of residential property.

What happens when you "borrow" money under the terms of a mortgage? Ownership of a dwelling is transferred when a deal is reached between buyer and seller. For most purchasers, the deal cannot be for cash. The vendor, however, cannot wait for 25 years to pocket the full price of his asset. By analysing what happens to resolve this dilemma, the myths are separated from reality.

▶ *As buyer*, you put down a deposit of (say) 10% of the purchase price. You need the difference to pay to the vendor. You go to a bank, which offers to "lend" you its money.

  – The reality: you sign an IOU. This is a pledge in which you promise that you will create value equal to 90% of the current sale price of the property.

  – For the next 25 years you set aside part of the value you create by your labour to redeem your pledge. At the end of that period, the IOU is scrapped. You are free of debt.

▶ *The vendor* receives the IOU. The pledge is deemed to be worth the value of the property. You become the owner of the house.

  – The vendor passes on the IOU by (say) purchasing another property, or investing it in stocks and shares, or spending it on holidays.

  – Credit in the economy (the "money" in circulation) has been increased by the value of your IOU.

▶ *Other people* need to be sure that you will not default on your pledge. Without that assurance, the IOU would be worthless, and therefore not transferrable. Your signature on the pledge, however, is not sufficient assurance to other people. They cannot trust you, because they do not know you personally.

  – Your pledge needs to be presented in a standardised format. This is achieved by the concept of "money". Now, all pledges may be exchanged on a like-for-like basis.

  – Government guarantees the face value of all the pledges, or IOUs. Your pledge goes into circulation as part of the money supply.

▶ *A remedy* is needed to deal with the risk of your defaulting. Your IOU's value rests on your agreement to create the value that will enable you to redeem it.

  – The deeds to your property are held by the bank. This (remember) is not collateral for the bank's "loan", since there was no such loan.

- If you fail to redeem your pledge, the property is repossessed and sold. The new owner's IOU replaces the one that you dishonoured. Total credit in circulation is maintained.

▶ *A mortgage* holding institution is needed as one of the parties to the transaction.

- An independent third party must verify that your income is sufficient to enable you to redeem your IOU. That is a clerical exercise that must be rewarded with a fee.

- Banks that provide such a service do *not* thereby acquire a legitimate right to a large slice of your future earnings in the form of "interest" on a non-existent "loan".

▶ *The guarantor* of the value of your IOU which has gone into circulation is the taxpayer. You. And me.

- Banks want us to believe that they stand behind the value of the credit in circulation. They do not. When banks became bankrupt in 2008, they were bailed out by government.

- Governments appear to be guarantors but, behind them, taxpayers are the ultimate insurers of the financial system. We the people are the guarantors of the credit which we create, and that credit rests on the value of our labour.

This way of viewing the money creation process is faithful to reality. It is the bedrock on which the money manipulators then proceed to construct their delusional activities, trading in "financial instruments" which turn out to be not worth the paper they are written on.

To sustain the realistic view of money creation, however, we have to exorcise the fictions that are embedded in our minds. One of these relates to the "interest" that is drained away from home buyers. The sums are huge – almost as much as the buying price of property that is transacted in the housing market (see Appendix 1 for the arithmetic of a typical transaction in Scotland). Roughly speaking, for every £1 that is paid to the vendor of the house, an additional £1 is gifted to the bank for doing nothing.

The sum that is called "interest" is part of the rent that accrues to the location on which a house is built. Consider what would happen if the payment of interest was outlawed (as some reform activists propose: see p.126). Would that value remain in the pockets of people buying houses? No! Prices would adjust in the market to consolidate that value into the cost of real estate. The increase in price would not be in favour of the bricks-and-mortar buildings, which depreciate with time. Those increases in value merge into the price of land (Box 3.2).

Box 3.2 **Paying off the bankers**

Money-lenders knew what they were doing, in the 16th century, when they joined the land grabbers to share the spoils of the public's finances. They captured part of the kingdom's rents, camouflaging their deeds by re-naming that income as "interest" on their "money". But to be fair, back then the function of money was assigned to precious metals: gold and silver. Arguably, the goldsmiths were entitled to a reward for handing over the gold and silver which they had accumulated as profits on their equity deals as merchants. Modern currencies, however, are backed by the value of people's labour. Banks, therefore, have no entitlement to a large and rising share of the nation's rents. They are entitled to no more than one-off fees for checking the credit worthiness of home buyers, and for providing a safe deposit for property deeds. That fee might be comparable (say) to the fee charged by surveyors who assess a property's value, or the fee charged by the lawyer who draws up the conveyancing documents.

The betrayal of integrity

Stewardship is a meaningless concept in the money-creating business. Responsibility for corrupt behaviour is deflected by attributing blame to rogue individuals. But financial crimes are not the result of a few "rotten apples". This became apparent in the five years that followed the financial explosion that was triggered by the malpractice of sub-prime mortgages. These rogue mortgages were sanctioned by the banks and sold to people who could not afford them. They resulted in a collapse that wiped $7 trillion off home-owner equity in the US alone.[8] Then, on both sides of the Atlantic, the evidence poured out to expose the corrupt behaviour of financial institutions which had engaged in

▶ manipulation of foreign exchanges rates

▶ miss-selling toxic financial products, including mortgage-backed securities and insurance policies

▶ rigging the interbank interest rate (LIBOR), to profit by deception in a $350tn market in financial instruments known as derivatives

▶ insider trading, to profit from privileged information at the expense of shareholders

▶ money laundering that helped clients to evade taxes in their country of domicile

▶ Ponzi schemes, such as the notorious racket orchestrated by Bernard Madoff

This is a portrait of what is meant by the "free market" in the propaganda circles which claim that the City of London is central to the health of the UK economy. Each of the multi-billion dollar rackets reveals a cynicism that was sanctioned

---

8 Anjli Raval (2014), "US housing: Battle scars", *Financial Times*, August 12.

by the cultural ethos embedded in High Finance. Governments are not capable of erasing that culture, because it is the product of centuries of acculturation. The cynicism and acquisitiveness of those engaged in "making money out of money" is vitriolic, corroding the attitudes of employees. There was one way only to deal with the corruption that had to come to the public's notice after 2008, and that was to sign cathartic deals wrapped up around financial settlements. In the five years up to the end of 2014, the costs of fines and litigation incurred by a group of the biggest global banks exceeded £200bn ($306bn) – a number that continued to rise with yet further fines in 2015.[9] JP Morgan alone paid an estimated $28.7bn over a 3-year period.[10] The impact was fourfold.

1. Bankers who failed to honour their duty of care to clients avoided gaol.
2. Banks were free to rebuild their finances and continue operating.
3. In most cases, the deals came with no admission of corporate guilt.
4. The something-for-nothing culture was preserved intact. None of the public enquiries scrutinised the cultural context which motivates people to behave corruptly.

Joe Public was left stunned. Why had no-one been held to account for the events within the Royal Bank of Scotland, which was rescued at a cost to Britain's taxpayers of £45bn? Vince Cable, a cabinet minister in Cameron's Coalition Government, did ask that question. A legal report prepared for him identified "prosecutable evidence" against several executives.[11] As the years dragged by, costs carried by the public grew bigger and frustration grew deeper. The guardians of the public's welfare trimmed their actions to accommodate rent-seeking values. An audit of the outcome leaves us in no doubt about the privileged protection of that culture of greed.

▶ The financial crisis was good business for the global banks. Fines were eclipsed by taxpayer-funded subsidies worth about $590bn, according to the IMF.[12]

▶ To fund those subsidies, governments imposed "austerity" on citizens. The human costs, in lost jobs and homes, psycho-social stresses and the degrading of communities, are impossible to quantify in cash terms.

Financiers had little to fear. They had tamed democracy by corrupting the norms of transparency and accountability. The manner in which they enjoy privileged access to the public purse is most unashamedly displayed in the United States. In Washington, money speaks loud and clear. According to the *New York Times*, austerity did not inhibit that nexus of interests identified by the FIRE acronym: "Lobbying expenditures by every specific industry group declined in

9 Ben McLannahan (2015), "Banks' post-crisis legal costs hit £200bn", *Financial Times*, June 8.
10 Dominic Rushe (2014), "JP Morgan pays $2bn over Madoff's scams", *The Guardian*, January 8.
11 James Chapman (2015), "Cable: Why have RBS bankers not been prosecuted?" *Daily Mail*, January 31.
12 International Monetary Fund (2014), *Global Financial Stability Report*, Washington DC, pp. 114-118.

2014, except for the finance, insurance and real estate sector. That sector increased its spending by 2.5 percent".[13]

Lone Rangers cannot loot wealth on an epic scale. They have to be aided and abetted by corruption which begins and ends with the rent-fuelled linkages between privileged power and the public purse. Bankers enjoy immunity for their actions, and a slice of the nation's rents, because of the 16th century deal to bankroll the aristocrats. Out of those land-and-money deals evolved one of the most lucrative scams: funding revenue-starved governments. Budgetary deficits were inevitable, once the rents began to slush into private pockets. This incubated the irresponsible form of governance: paying for public services by transferring the costs on to future generations – aka "deficit spending".

The "too big to fail" doctrine survives because people lack the power to hold banks to account. Bankers oblige others to pay the costs of their irresponsible behaviour. This is the classic indicator of rent-seeking: costs are "externalised" onto others, while benefits go into private pockets. That nothing has changed since 2008 is confirmed by the fact that the relationship of people to the money system has been preserved.

▶ Families cannot acquire homes without securing the *permission* of banks. What will it take to remove that power exercised by banks over people's lives?

▶ Small- and medium-sized enterprises are denied the credit needed to rebuild their businesses. When will banks be deprived of that power over production?

High Finance continues to be motivated by the creed which encouraged one Barclays trader to berate his colleagues with these brutally honest words: "If you ain't cheating, you ain't trying!"[14] Governments cannot erase that culture of cheating because they do not exercise the power to do so. A large part of sovereign authority was ceded to financiers in the 16th century; the power over the territory which, from then onwards, would be administered by a statecraft of greed.

---

13 Jonathan Weisman and Eric Lipton, "In New Congress, Wall St. Pushes to Undermine Dodd-Frank Reform", *New York Times*, January 13, 2015.
14 Mark Odell (2015), "Trader transcripts: 'If you ain't cheating, you ain't trying'", *Financial Times*, May 20.

Baron Green of Hurstpierpoint (1948–)

The corporate intelligence of institutions that are culturally programmed to behave badly guides the selection of front men. A Man of God who is prepared to serve Mammon is perfect for a bank. Stephen Keith Green was a natural choice as the public face of HSBC, the third largest bank in the world as measured by assets. Green, a Church of England clergyman, served as Group Treasurer in 1992, was elevated to Group Chief Executive in 2003, and became Chairman in 2006. He resigned when he was offered a life peerage, and in 2011, as Baron Green of Hurstpierpoint, he joined the Cameron Coalition government as Minister of State for Trade and Investment.

Back in 2003, *Guardian* reporter Jill Treanor asked the Rev. Green how he reconciled HSBC's high salaries and bonuses with his religious faith. He replied: "Do I personally feel some kind of incompatibility between what I believe and being in financial services markets? I can only say no".[15] His beliefs would be strained as the bad news began to tumble out in the years of financial crisis.

 ▶ In July 2012 the US Senate's Permanent Subcommittee on Investigations released a 335-page report which alleged that HSBC had bypassed the USA's sanctions against Iran, and had facilitated money laundering by Mexican drug cartels. It had also conducted business with companies with links to terrorism. The report quoted emails which detailed those transactions, copies of which had been sent to Green.

 ▶ In February 2015, in a TV programme entitled *The Bank of Tax Cheats*, the BBC alleged that HSBC's Private Banking Holdings (Suisse) SA had helped more than 100,000 clients from over 200 countries to evade tax worth hundreds of millions of pounds. Green was the Swiss bank's chairman at the time of the alleged offences.

The revelations were embarrassing for Stephen Green. He had written a book in which he questioned *Serving God? Serving Mammon?* (1996). He sought to square his religious beliefs with the money-making ethic with this reasoning:

"Life in the markets is ambiguous, certainly...but so is life in other fields. Trading depends on an instinct for competitive gain but that is true of all human commerce. The competitive instinct can become obsessive and unbalanced but it's not intrinsically wrong...It needs to be fettered by law and regulation where

---

15 Jill Treanor (2003), "Preaching profit", *The Guardian*, October 18.

appropriate; and it needs to be developed within a shared moral framework which places public value on integrity in commercial practice and on care for the weak. Where these conditions prevail the competitive instinct is compatible with the basic commandment to love our neighbours as ourselves."

As the scandals began to make the headlines, exposing the corrupt deeds that had enabled financiers to enter the ranks of the richest citizens in the world, the reverend ruminated:

"Underlying all these events is a question about the culture and ethics of the industry. It is as if, too often, people had given up asking whether something was the right thing to do, and focused only whether it was legal and complied with the rules. The industry needs to recover a sense of what is right and suitable as a key impulse for doing business."[16]

The Reverend and Right Honourable Prebendary had still not grasped the organising principle of modern culture. How could it be otherwise? Claims to money in the form of interest may be held in bad odour in the sacred texts of the three Abrahamic faiths, but they are sanctioned by the UN Declaration of Universal Human Rights and the European Conventions on Human Rights. And, anyway, the British government's tax collecting agency (HMRC) had been provided with the evidence of what HSBC was up to in 2010, and had failed to intervene. Only when the stories make headlines do the authorities take action, and the culture of cheating has elevated censorship into an art. We can therefore conclude that corruption will continue as a systemic reality in the financial sector in the 21st century.

In 2015, HSBC paid $43m in compensation to resolve the money-laundering investigation in Switzerland and recovered its money by announcing it would sack 4,000 of its employees in the UK and redeploy the jobs to Asia where costs were lower. It also began to review the location of its headquarters in the search for more congenial regulatory climes. Making money, after all, was the name of the game.

HSBC's failures were no worse than the other banks. How the unequal relationship between bank and citizen can be altered will be considered in Part III. But first, we need to unravel the dynamics of cultural cannibalism.

---

16 Russell Lynch (2009), "HSBC in bid to raise £12.5bn", *Independent*, March 2.

Part II

Cultural Cannibalism

4

Cheating as Social Process

RENT-SEEKING is an existential threat to humanity. It undermines an authentically people-centred culture by draining the creative energy out of the population. Once the virus has taken hold in its host population, the challenge must be resolved on life-or-death terms. For the duration of that contest, society becomes the site of civil conflict. Winner takes all. Half measures and compromises are not possible, because rent-seeking is by its nature cannibalistic. It necessarily consumes the vitality of those who add the value to the wealth of their communities. That wealth is the material basis of the psycho-social and spiritual condition of the people. Rent-seeking culture consumes those resources, without which humanity is debased. Rent-seeking, once it controls the levers in the junction boxes of the social system, must systematically impoverish a population at all levels of existence. Humanity is its enemy.

Imperfections in the way of life in the United Kingdom today are not accidental. Nor can they be treated as a lack of ingenuity on the part of the people. The explanation is to be found in the logic of the cheating virus which mutated from the narcissistic inclinations of a few people into its institutionalised forms.

Cheating with a social purpose.

For that kind of cheating to flourish, it must acquire sufficient power to disarm the population, defeating the remedial measures that rational people would otherwise adopt in defence of their interests. In other words, I claim that the people of Britain, for all the power that they were supposed to have acquired through the onset of universal suffrage, are not in control of their destiny.

This proposition is offensive to common sensibilities. Does the evidence demonstrate that the UK is in the grip of what originated as a killing cult and survived by cannibalising the English and all of those peoples who fell under the sway of the Empire?

To sustain my thesis, I have to offer the level of proof that meets the tests applied in a court of law. For guilt to be established, it is not sufficient to show that an act took place with damaging outcomes. The perpetrator might have been innocent of the consequences of his actions. The prosecution has to demonstrate *intent*. The evidence must demonstrate that the quest to capture the nation's rents was the motivating force of a culture which intentionally deprived people of the freedom to fashion the quality of life of their choice.

Joel Hurstfield, the late professor of history at University College, London, defined the test that we must meet.

"If we assume that the object of the State is the welfare of all its members, we may define corruption as the subversion of that object for other ends."[1]

Does the British State under-mine people's welfare to enrich a privileged section of society? Hurstfield emphasised that, in relation to governance and the State, corruption entailed more than just the exchange of money. He specified three levels of corruption.

1. Bribes that are accepted while holding judicial office.
2. The State is damaged when its revenues benefit private persons.
3. Appointment and advancement in public service are by favouritism, or for reasons other than the public interest.

All three levels of corruption featured in the evolution of the English State. This could not happen independently of the use and abuse of State revenues. The history of politics and High Finance reveals the intent of the cultural architects who were the principal beneficiaries. Past deeds of corruption now dictate the options of the Welfare State.

To illuminate the evolution of the culture of institutionalised cheating, we need to excavate the evidence which exposes how

▶ revenue which ought to have gone into the public purse was redirected into private pockets. And

▶ as a consequence, the welfare of the population was fatally damaged.

In England, was there a causal relationship between class-based ideology, the formation of State institutions and the disposition of the public's finances, in a way that proves beyond doubt that the people suffered on a socially significant scale?

Disconnecting the English

At the centre of the culture of rent-seeking was the formation of the post-feudal class of nobility. Social historian E.P. Thompson summarised the chief character-istic of that privileged group:

"The landed gentry are graded less by birth or other marks of status than by rentals: they are worth so many thousand pounds a year. Among the aristocracy and ambi-tious gentry, courtship is conducted by fathers and by their lawyers, who guide it carefully towards its consummation, the well-drawn marriage settlement.

---

1 Joel Hurstfield (1967), "Political Corruption in Modern England", *History*, Vol. LII(174), p.19.

Place and office could be bought and sold (provided that the sale did not seriously conflict with the lines of political interest); commissions in the Army; sets in Parliament. Use-rights, privileges, liberties, service – all could be translated into an equivalent in money: votes, burgage-rights, immunities from parish office or militia service...A dove-cot on the site of an ancient burgage may be sold, and with it is sold a right to vote; the rubble of an ancient messuage may be bought up in support of a claim for common right and, thereby, of an extra allocation of the common on enclosure."[2]

That class wilfully privatised the rents which Marshall called the *public value*. That process found its physical expression in the formation of the class which we generically classify as rent-seekers. The damage they caused is schematically traced in the graphic below.

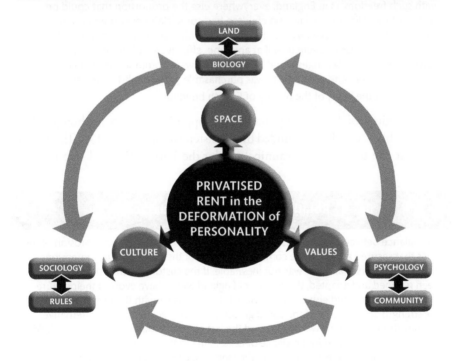

The pathology of personality deformation

LAND
BIOLOGY
SPACE
PRIVATISED RENT in the DEFORMATION of PERSONALITY
CULTURE
VALUES
SOCIOLOGY
RULES
PSYCHOLOGY
COMMUNITY

▶ By channelling rents away from their social uses, communities were impoverished as the primary value system was debased. Collective consciousness – the psychology of the population – was malformed to accommodate the loss of the rents.

---

2 E.P. Thompson (1991), *Customs in Common*, London: Penguin, pp.24-25.

▶ The transmission mechanisms for rent privatisation re-configured people's spatial relationships. As access to the natural environment was eroded, the instinct-based capacity to use the landscape as a reference manual (a mental map) was blunted. Behaviour was disorientated.

▶ As the State-enforced rules were changed to favour rent-seeking, culture and habitats were damaged. Dysfunctional adjustments were synchronised through the feedback loops within the social system.

One outcome was the individualism that is eulogised as an achievement of the people of Britain. Interpreting that characteristic through an examination of the buildings constructed over the past thousand years, Simon Thurley, a professor of the built environment and head of English Heritage claims:

"A central feature of English social structure is the rights and privileges of the individual over the group and over the state. This leads to a particular view of property rights. Nowhere else in Western Europe could an owner dispose of his property with such freedom as in England; everywhere else the proportion that could be freely sold was limited by law and children had some claim over their parents' property. In England, even with primogeniture, which became the rule from the 16th century, it was possible to sell at any time, effectively disinheriting the following generation. So English land and buildings were commodities that could be easily transferred, and all property was purchasable. Individualistic property ownership lies at the heart of the history of English building."[3]

That reading of history appears on the opposite page to a photograph of Rievaulx Abbey, which was founded by 12 Cistercian monks in 1132. The caption notes that the building was cannibalised by the Earl of Rutland. He used the

---

Box 4.1 Rotating fields rooted in social solidarity

The balance between individuals and their groups was dislocated by the erosion of the rules that secured access to the commons. Erosion of the group's social dimensions – and people's personalities – was not inevitable. If the customs of the commons had been retained and adapted, the people of England would have evolved their culture in ways that combined enhanced individual characteristics with the preservation of the strength and integrity of the social group. We may speculate on this alternative journey through time by walking around the last surviving example of the three-field system, which is located in the village of Laxton, in Nottinghamshire.

Laxton, whose name is recorded in the Domesday Book, retains the open field system. The fields, divided into strips, are rotated between 14 tenants who use the land according to practices extending back to medieval times. The outcome is not anachronistic: common access has been adapted to take advantage of economic opportunities and modern technologies. The farmers continue to participate in the governance of the land through the Court Leet, through which they hold each other responsible for their actions.

---

3 Simon Thurley (2013), *The Building of England*, London: William Collins, p.15.

stones to construct his stately home and establish his petty fiefdom in Yorkshire, the better to exercise power over the communities that fell within his domain. This happened all over England, following the sacrilegious intervention of Henry VIII in the 1530s. Over 800 religious communities disappeared in the space of 20 years. As the aristocracy constructed palatial monuments to their dynastic egos out of the debris of the spiritual life of the nation, the social networks that circulated around the religious houses were torn apart. People-centred communities were replaced by the power-centred culture that celebrated the narcissism of the patricians. This was the self-centred "individualism" that trampled on society (Box 4.1).

Waves of cultural de-formation

English history over the past 500 years is generally viewed in sympathetic terms as the evolution of a culture of progress. The alternative interpretation, based on the intrusive influence of those who appropriated the public value, highlights the incubation of a psychotic culture. This mutated through three stages.

Stage 1

The primary disconnection of peasants from their natural habitats, engineered through land enclosures and the erasure of common tenure rights.

▶ Landscape reference points which guided people through the seasons and ensured viable household economics were degraded.

▶ Folk culture, which guided people through the generations, became ineffective, was questioned, and then emaciated rather than renewed.

Stage 2

The depersonalising of relationships, through the imposition of a doctrine of material values, vaporised the moral economy.

▶ Intimate relationships between people and the products of their labour were severed by pressures that drove them into the cash economy.

▶ Personal responsibility was replaced by a legal calculus that enabled people in power to claim they had clean hands.

Stage 3

The doctrine of social progress was imposed to persuade people to accept the notion that no-one was being victimised.

▶ Social outcasts were schooled into accepting their subordinate "place" in the new order.

▶ The State protected the elites in ways that made it safe, in due course, to allow the veneer of participative politics.

With a few exceptions, philosophers reinforced this trend by glossing over the shortcomings in a period in European history known as the Enlightenment. People were encouraged to believe that they were free to think, and even to speak out in public; providing, of course, that they conformed to the social roles assigned to them.

This broad sweep of history needs to be understood in terms of the formation of the culture of irresponsibility as it was applied at both the personal and institutional levels. The contours of three waves are visible.

Wave 1

▶ *Personal irresponsibility:* in the 16th century the feudal aristocrats accelerated the perversion of the power of the State by privatising the income that traditionally funded public services. This larceny was accomplished by corrupting the institutions of governance. This, consequently, fostered

▶ *institutionalised irresponsibility:* over the 17th and 18th centuries, laws and political practices were fashioned to separate the nation's territory from the people who laboured on it. This mutated into Wave 2.

Wave 2

▶ *Personal irresponsibility:* in the 19th century, the attractions of the rent-seeking culture co-opted the middle class, and especially the Captains of Industry who sought entry into the ranks of the nobility.

▶ *Institutionalised irresponsibility:* the banking system was shaped to aid and abet the deficits of the State and acquisitive needs of land owners. Again, this mutated into the next round.

Wave 3

▶ *Institutionalised irresponsibility:* the 20th century was heralded as the Age of the Common Man. But universal suffrage was managed to ensure that people remained within the limits tolerated by the culture of greed. This ensnared everyone into the age of

▶ *personal irresponsibility:* the 21st century dawned as the age in which even low-income people were encouraged to adopt the habits of rent-seekers by signing up for capital gains from land, extracted from sub-prime mortgages.

The taming of time

The absolute power of the rent-seeking aristocracy was displayed in the way they came to control the nation's time.

In evolutionary terms, humans learnt how to graft social time onto the rhythms shaped by the laws of nature. They integrated rituals into the climatic seasons, gradually merging their mental universe with the natural universe. The outcome was something uniquely human: the social galaxy. The timing of marriages, the affirmation of authority structures, the organisation of joyous festivals…all were spun around the rhythms of time that served everyone's interests. Then the aristocracy made their bid to control the nation's rents. They could not convert that revenue into their private property without taking control of social time. Time horizons had to be completely redesigned. Time was converted into power and money, at the expense of those who were separated from the public value which they created.

Primogeniture fashioned the first step into the realms of the timeless timetable. The practice of passing land down through the eldest son was adopted in the 16th century to buy the time for noble families to consolidate power over the public purse. Time had to be stretched so that the aristocracy could erode the monarch's authority and transfer into their hands the powers of the State. Time was needed to accumulate sufficient resources on which to rest their personal power. And they needed time to degrade the folk customs and practices that bolstered the lives of the peasants. This meant one thing: land had to be held in large, single parcels. This secured the concentration of decision-making in the hands of a few people, who could accumulate sufficient funds to construct the monumental buildings that would symbolise unchallengeable power. Grass for grazing sheep and cattle was the primary source of rent. Grass took time to grow. Gold was the physical embodiment of money. Gold could not be manufactured, and took time to accumulate. Time was what the nobility needed, and they fashioned it by locking the nation into the rhythms dictated by the tenure that suited their goals: primogeniture.

By this means, minds were altered. Self-consciousness was transformed. Oil paintings on ancestral walls conveyed the identities of the privileged families through the centuries, as each generation reminded itself of its superiority. Meanwhile, the peasants who were vanquished from the commons, or scattered because their hamlets were demolished to make way for game parks, suffered an attrition of the mind. Collective memories were lost as the fabric of their villages were torn apart, children forced to migrate, physical exhaustion reducing the opportunities to organise the community rituals that linked past with future generations.

Then, as industry supplanted agriculture in importance, time was allowed to speed up. Tenure had to be modified to keep pace with the new opportunities. Layers of rents were being ripped out of the earth, capital gains accumulated by trading in small parcels of land to feed the new urbanisation of the 19th century. Family fortunes grew bigger as portfolios were diversified into new sectors. To accommodate the tenure/time nexus of the rent-seekers, bodies were altered. In place of the rhythms of the diversified household economy in rural areas, families were reduced to monotonous mono-cultures: taking in the wool to spin for merchants, congregating in large factories to feed the conveyor belts, all the time watching the master's clock.

As the labour force was increasingly congealed into clogs and cloth caps, the lesser nobility exploited personal influence for financial and status preferment through the institutions of the State. This was "the world of patronage and place of the older professionals, particularly the Law and the Church, and the older type of merchant and financier…This is the meaning of the extraordinarily high percentage of early wealth-holders, particularly those among the 'lesser wealthy' deceased in 1809-29, engaged in the professions, public administration and the military".[4]

Table 4.1 **Occupation of wealth-holders: UK**					
		1809-58	**1858-79**	**1880-99**	**1900-14**
Millionaires	**Land**	181	117	38	27
	Others*	9	30	59	73
Half-millionaires	**Land**	349	165	137	80
	Others	48	101	158	181

* Manufacturing; Food, Drink & Tobacco; Commercial; Professional, Public Administration & Defence
Source: W.D. Rubinstein (1977), "Wealth, Elites and the Class Structure of Modern Britain", *Past & Present*, No. 76, Table 1, p.102.

By the end of the 18th century, seven-eighths of all persons worth over £100,000 were landowners. During most of the 19th century (Table 4.1), by far the majority of the richest people in the kingdom extracted their income from others via the rent of land. The numbers appeared to change in favour of value-adding occupations after the Corn Laws were abolished in the 1830s. Two facts stand out from this history, however, which confirm that Britain entered the modern era as a predominantly land-owning culture. Rent-seeking remained in control into the 20th century.

1. Until the 1880s, more than half of Britain's wealthiest men were land-owners. They were far richer than the richest businessmen. Dukes who owned London real estate were worth upwards of £14m, whereas legacies of the wealthiest businessmen were no more than £6m.

2. Despite the Industrial Revolution, most of the wealth accumulated by those in the other economic categories was not generated by manufacturing. It came from commerce and finance. Finance meant banking and stock-broking, which was heavily engaged in extracting part of the nation's rents (Ch. 3, see pp.42-43).

The data in Table 4.1 understates the bias that favoured rent-seeking. Descendants of businessmen who were *rentiers* were assigned to the category in which

---

4 W.D. Rubinstein (1977), "Wealth, Elites and the Class Structure of Modern Britain", *Past & Present*, No. 76, p. 118.

the family fortune had originally been made.[5] The second- and third-generation offspring of merchants or industrialists did not recycle much of their wealth back into manufacturing or commercial enterprises; they ploughed their money into country estates. The time-and-tenure syndrome that underpins those estates continues to shape the public discourse to this day (Box 4.2).

Box 4.2 **Snared in a time warp**

The 13th Duke of Argyle was outraged. The SNP government had announced it would consult on changing the law to enable all children to inherit land in Scotland. Allowing landowners' close relatives to inherit land was "terrifying". This would make it impossible to sustain castles like his family seat at Inveraray. "Would you give one person the castle and the other person the land? And then the person who has got the castle cannot run the castle because he hasn't got any money. It takes a generation or two and the whole thing has gone. It is terrifying," he told the *Financial Times* (June 27, 2015).

It was not just the peasant whose life was altered forever by the rent-seeking culture. The "captains of industry" were rare creatures in the land that invented factory-based mass production. Narcissistic inclinations overshadowed the value-adding motive. Making money the easy way was more attractive than making products for sale to consumers. By 1866, the media had concluded that "the City [of London] is rapidly becoming another branch of that system of relief for the aristocracy", in contrast to industry, which possessed few such attractions for the sons of noble families.[6]

The Industrial Revolution failed to dissolve the power of the rent-seekers. Rubinstein notes that the middle class located in London was "far closer to the old society than its provincial counterpart". While industrial workers of the North engaged in near-insurrection behaviour from about 1790 to 1845, the middle class of London was notable for its absence – "the invisibility of this class was its failure to join in reform agitation" from the 1780s through to the Jarrow hunger-marches of the 1930s. The only way to account for this was the aspiration to join the rent-seeking class via petty land ownership – the acquisition of the small plot beneath "the Englishman's castle", the family residence. Patience paid off: by the 21st century, most of the wealth of the nation was held by the middle-class home-owner of London and the South-east.

Today, the cultural folly which bankrupted the profligate sons of 19th century merchants is still draining the vitality out of the British economy. One investment manager has noted how investors were damaging entrepreneurialism because they had "sunk all spare capital into a house, and are so heavily geared [indebted] as to make borrowing any more simply too risky a prospect. This does not bode well

---

5 Rubinstein (1977), p.102, n.8.
6 Rubinstein (1977), pp.114-115.

for the British business in the future".[7] The culture of cheating had triumphed. The "baby boomers" are cannibalising the lives of their grand-children, by switching assets from the stock market (where savings could be invested in job-creating, value-adding enterprises) to buy-to-let residential properties. The new generation of landlords pocketed £112bn in the 12 months to May 2015, which raised the value of their property to $1 trillion. This, observed the chief executive of one bank, meant that "Buy-to-let has come of age, moving from a niche asset class to one big enough to rival the stock market".[8]

The misallocation of capital and labour talent continues to drain the creativity of the UK economy. City bankers are using their bonuses to ape the nobility. They have become what the *Financial Times* called the "'lifestyle buyers' attracted by the prospect of breeding horses or building a big house" in the countryside.[9] Over the decade to 2015, the rate of increase in prime agricultural land values outstripped the increase in the value of any other class of asset.

Moulding the compliant personality

The peoples of the British Isles are imbued with a powerful sense of fair play. The culture of cheating could only prevail by re-moulding their minds into a state of acquiescence. There can be no doubt as to who did the moulding. Cambridge University historian Peter Laslett emphasised that, in pre-industrial England, "there were a large number of status groups but only one body of persons capable of concerted action over the whole area of society".[10] Their aspirations could only be achieved by the initiation of a two-step intrusion into the collective consciousness of the population.

- ▶ Spatial dominance was the crucial first step. To take command, the territory has to be dominated before those living on it can be exploited.
  - – Monopolising the land gives control over people's biological survival, turning them into servile dependents.
  - – Dependent people have no choice but to yield the product over and above their wages, which is the rents they create.
- ▶ To enjoy their spoils, in time the rent-seekers had to swap tools of violence for cost-effective techniques for neutralising opposition.
  - – Bending the language leads to mind control, disarming people, dislocating them from reality. The concepts of "land" and "rent" were eliminated from the diagnostic toolkit of economists.
  - – Co-opting the social outcasts into the culture of greed is achieved by dangling the prospect of sharing the spoils.

---

7 Simon Evan-Cook (2015), "Would-be entrepreneurs have sunk their capital into high-prices homes", Letter, *Financial Times*, May 4.
8 Anna White (2015), "Value of property held by landlords hits £990bn", *Daily Telegraph*, May 29.
9 Scheherazade Daneshkhu (2015), "Farmland proves fertile for investors", *Financial Times*, February 19.
10 Peter Laslett (1965), *The World we have Lost*, London: Methuen, pp.22.

This process was dragged out over four centuries. By their control over the land, the aristocracy exercised the over-whelming power to embed the norms of their narcissistic culture.

E.P. Thompson notes that it was in the 18th century that "the commoners finally lost their land, in which the number of offences carrying the capital penalty multiplied, in which thousands of felons were transported, and in which thousands of lives were lost in imperial wars; a century which ended, despite the agricultural 'revolution' and the swelling rent-rolls, in severe rural immiseration".[11] Bludgeoned into this pitiful state, the people of Britain were putty in the hands of the rent-seekers. From then on, "soft power" could be used to control the population. This was "the manufacture of consent".[12]

The language of politics, with terms like "the poor" attached to the dispossessed, engrained humiliation in the psyches of vanquished peasants. Demeaning labels were supplemented to create the impression of paternalism on the part of the land-grabbers and their descendants. Thompson notes that "Cultural hegemony of this kind induces exactly such a state of mind in which the established structures of authority and modes of exploitation appear to be in the very course of nature".

Social outcasts were schooled into publicly acknowledging their subordinate status through gestures of deference to their "betters". That deference polluted the mind-set of factory workers in the 19th century, with employees (notwithstanding the rise of trades unions) aligning their interests with those of their employers and against the employees at rival factories.

Morality was compromised, an essential device to inhibit the losers from searching for support from alternative sources of authority. The State, and the "rule of law", set the standards of acceptable behaviour, so there was no question of censuring the rent-seekers for their impact on society.

Aesthetic sensibilities were refashioned to accommodate the tastes of the aristocrats who patronised the artists. To escape such dependency, an artist or skilled craftsman sought to "purchase immunity from deference by acquiring the wealth which would give him 'independence', or land and gentry status".

The presence in public of the aristocracy took the form of "theatre" in its many forms (in law courts, on sporting occasions, and so on) to continuously remind people of their subordinate social roles. The net effect was the collective humiliation of the social outcasts (Box 4.3). That this social pathology is being propagated in the 21st century may be inferred from the use of concepts like *gentrification*. That word signifies the mechanism whereby low-income families are displaced from locations coveted by higher-income earners. Gentrification is the economics of apartheid in action: the land grab in the modern urban context, securing separate development on the basis of the culture of rent-seeking.

---

11 Thompson (1991), Ch.2.
12 Edward S. Herman and Noam Chomsky (1994), *Manufacturing Consent*, London: Vintage.

The in-migrants have the means to anticipate future capital gains from land, while the out-migrants are displaced into less advantageously endowed locations.

The outcome of this history was a weakened sovereign State. This was the direct result of power over the public value being transferred to landowners and their financiers. All the changes in behaviour that made possible that shift in power undermined the State's role as guardian of the welfare of the whole population. This meets the tests specified by Joel Hurstfield to denote corruption. The result is corrupted culture that denies the people of England full control over their destiny.

Box 4.3 **The theatre of degradation**

Language was adjusted as a primary tool for creating and preserving the economics of apartheid. The World Bank illustrates a current case: the caste system in India. Low-caste boys were as competent at solving puzzles as high-caste boys when caste identity was not revealed. In mixed-caste groups, however, revealing the boys' castes before puzzle-solving sessions resulted in stigmatized low-caste boys under-performing high-caste boys by 23%.[1]

In colonial settings, white plantation owners combined language with physical posturing to dominate black workers, to establish the superior/inferior relationship. That language survives in one Melanesia post-colonial country, elevated into the language of governance, religion and communication.[2] Using language to differentiate between rich and poor remains intrinsic to the recruitment practices of the UK's elite financial services and legal firms, which tend to bias their selection of employees on the basis of class-conscious language.[3]

1 World Bank (2015), *Mind, Society, and Behavior*, Washington, DC: World Bank, p.12.
2 Nikolas Coupland and Adam Jaworski (1997), *Sociolinguists*, London: Macmillan, p.29.
3 Louise Ashley *et. al.* (2015), *A qualitative evaluation of non-educational barriers to the elite professions*, London: Social Mobility and Child Poverty Commission.

Sir Nicholas Stern (1946–)

To protect itself, the rent-seeking culture had to provide lightning conductors to attract and diffuse the frustration of its victims. Political space was allowed for criticisms that did not threaten the fortunes derived from Land-lordism. An effective distraction was Capital-ism. Obligingly, Karl Marx focused workplace discontent on the owners of factories. "The market" is demonised for causing the traumas inflicted on working people. "Market failure" is now the favoured explanation for unemployment, the income gap dividing rich from poor, unaffordable housing…just about everything. The concept of failure, however, has two meanings: *breakdown* and *blameability*.

Under the influence of rent-seeking, breakdowns in market activity are not failures in the blameability sense. They are due to distorted financial incentives licensed by government.

▶ The public pricing mechanism was rigged by the English aristocracy to privilege the interests of those with the power to extract a share of the nation's rents.

▶ The private pricing mechanism was fixed to "externalise" some of the costs of production. Transferring costs onto others increases the flow of rents into the land market.

Governments could change those incentives. But identifying imperfections in the character of taxation is disallowed. That is why Sir Nicholas Stern got into trouble with Her Majesty's Treasury.

They do not come more distinguished in the realm of academia than Nicholas Stern. As a professor of economics at the London School of Economics, his teaching credentials are impeccable. He was elected President of the prestigious British Academy in 2013, and his trustworthiness as a citizen of the United Kingdom is attested by his five years' service as head of the UK Government Economic Service. His reputation as a man of integrity led to his election as an Honorary Fellow of the American Academy of Arts and Sciences and Foreign Honorary Member of the American Economic Association.

So why did the British Government decide to gag him?

During his tenure as a servant of the Crown, Stern produced three reports. One was on climate change. The second was for the Commission for Africa. These were acclaimed, so HM Treasury had no qualms about Stern writing a report on taxation. He duly submitted his report. Mysteriously, it disappeared. It was not published. Why?

Stern made one mistake. He broke the taboo. *He dared to interrogate the financial algorithm that is the source of political power.* His conclusions were explosive. The report was locked away in a cabinet as a Secret of State. But the State had a problem. Parliament enacted the Freedom of Information Act (2000). This required public agencies to disclose information under due process of law. A request was lodged for Stern's report to be disclosed under the law sponsored by Tony Blair's New Labour Government.

That law was a "blunder", in Blair's word, which he lived to regret. "You idiot," he wrote in his autobiography. "You naive, foolish, irresponsible nincompoop. There is really no description of stupidity, no matter how vivid, that is adequate. I quake at the imbecility of it."[13]

---

13 Tony Blair (2011), *A Journey*, London: Arrow Books, p.516.

Blair need not have worried. The guardians of the culture of rent-seeking were not going to relent. So sensitive did they deem the contents of Stern's report that HM Treasury *refused to even confirm that the document existed*. The letter of rejection declared that "we consider that the wider public interest lies in neither confirming nor denying that information, which may have been disclosed in an unauthorised manner..."[14]

Had the professor revealed sensitive information that could be used by an enemy of the State? Had he disclosed secrets that would give comfort to (say) jihadi fundamentalists? Had he compromised anti-terrorist operations and endangered the lives of agents of Her Majesty's Secret Service? No! His was a far graver crime. In analysing High Finance, he dared to address the issue of how best to fund the public's services.

Stern's patience finally broke. He decided to flout time-honoured convention. The stiff English upper lip quivered. He disclosed his frustration in an article in the *Financial Times*, in which he revealed the one nugget of information that was not supposed to be aired in public:

"Far better to base taxation on the value of land – which, unlike other assets, cannot be spirited offshore. We urgently need a thoroughgoing review of housing and land taxation."[15]

Stern had to be silenced. Deploying the time-honoured excuse – "the public interest" – the principle of transparency was brusquely shoved aside. Accountability was also dishonoured to protect the culture that was abusing the people who laboured to create the wealth of the nation.

The censoring of Sir Nicolas Stern illuminates a grotesque reality. Agencies of the State are at the disposal of a vitriolic culture that dissolves the moral foundations of society. Sir Nicholas got into trouble with HM Treasury because he thought his job was to provide an honest account of taxation.

---

14 Email letter to Carol Wilcox from Fay Wiltshire, "Freedom of Information Act 2000: Sir Nicholas Stern's report on the reform of the tax system", Information Rights Unit, HM Treasury, 16 December, 2014.
15 Nicholas Stern (2014), "Fairer fixes for the public purse in a chancellor's draw", *Financial Times*, August 6.

5

Of Zombies and Zealots

ON February 23, 2006, George Osborne revealed to the world why he was not fit to hold high office in Her Majesty's Government. His incompetence was disclosed on the rostrum in University College Dublin's School of Business, when he said:

> "A generation ago, the very idea that a British politician would go to Ireland to see how to run an economy would have been laughable. The Irish Republic was seen as Britain's poor and troubled country cousin, a rural backwater on the edge of Europe. Today things are different. Ireland stands as a shining example of the art of the possible in long-term economic policymaking, and that is why I am in Dublin: to listen and to learn...What has caused this Irish miracle, and how can we in Britain emulate it?"

Osborne is a member of the political class of zealots who believe they are masters of the skills that entitle them to steer the Ships of State. Even as he spoke, the dials were on Red Alert. The Irish economy was ready to explode.

Osborne did not have the faintest idea of what was happening beneath his feet. And the economists in the Business School were not about to enlighten him. The consensus in Dublin was that the Celtic Tiger did, indeed, have much to teach the Member from the Parliament in Westminster. They were as blinkered as he was. They were not in the business of decoding the data that is charted in Graph 5.1. House prices were approaching their peak. That peak, as I had been forecasting since 1997, would be achieved in 2007, and it would be followed by a devastating depression.

Two researchers, Karl Deeter and Frank Quinn, diligently combed thousands of property records in the archives in Dublin to compile the data on which the graph is constructed. They based the values on the year 1900. That flattened the amplitudes of the booms and busts over the course of 300 years, but it had the advantage of dramatising the cauldron that was boiling away at the heart of the Irish economy in the decade up to 2007.

Throughout this period sufficient evidence was available to alert the politicians. They had the time to take remedial action. The volcanic eruption in the housing market need not have happened. They failed to act because Ireland, in common with other countries in Europe, was governed by zombie political parties. As institutions, they had become irresponsible and unaccountable. They exist to acquire power as the end in itself; then to administer the managed chaos in pursuit of re-election. Those parties had forfeited the trust of their people. They retained power because the political game is played according to the rules of musical chairs. So the zombies continued to rule, ever-ready to replenish their ranks with yet more zealots. Like George Osborne. Three years later he became Chancellor of the Exchequer and keeper of the UK's finances.

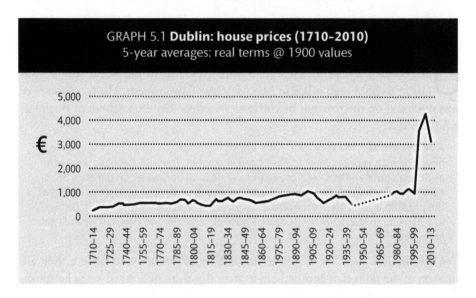

GRAPH 5.1 **Dublin: house prices (1710–2010)**
5-year averages: real terms @ 1900 values

Osborne was not alone in singing the praises of the Celtic Tiger. In 2008, the annual Index of Economic Freedom, compiled by the Heritage Foundation and *The Wall Street Journal*, ranked Ireland third in the world (behind Hong Kong and Singapore) in its assessment of the link between economic opportunity and prosperity, and no less than *first* out of 41 countries in the European region.[1] Yet the housing market had already turned down and the banks were on the verge of imploding. Two years later the government and its bankrupt banks would be bailed out by the European Union (EU) and the International Monetary Fund (IMF). But the economic ideologues were still applauding what Osborne called Ireland's model of "long-term economic policymaking".

In Paris, the Organisation for Economic Cooperation and Development (OECD) runs an expensive monitoring operation on behalf of 34 member nations. It, too, was not in the business of alerting the government in Dublin. Chief economist Pier Carlo Padoan confessed that "predictions are very difficult; especially

---

1 Kim R. Holmes *et al* (2008), *Index of Economic Freedom*, Washington, DC: Heritage Foundation, p.219.

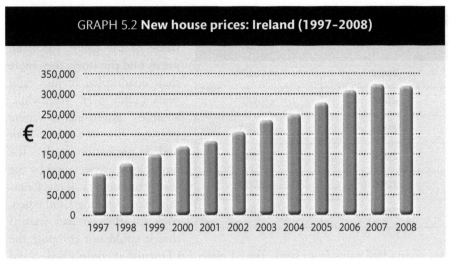

GRAPH 5.2 **New house prices: Ireland (1997–2008)**

Source: Building Industry Bulletin (2009).

if they are about the future…it is particularly true with economic forecasts".[2] The OECD failed to anticipate the 2008 crisis because its macro-economic model excluded the banking sector. The equations also excluded land prices. So the world at large was lulled by the reassurance that all was well. The toxic brew was free to bubble away unseen until the land market was ready to collapse and drag the banks down with it. Not everyone suffered. As his reward, a few months after his confession of failure Mr Padoan was elevated to finance minister of Italy.

The zealots use inducements (some would call them bribes) – with cash from the public purse – to retain control. In Ireland, one such episode occurred prior to the election in 1997, at the beginning of the new land-led property cycle. The prospect was offered of abolishing the property tax on people's homes – in return, of course, for votes. According to the authorised version, this would animate the psychology of the population: house prices would rise, people would feel wealthy, more money would be spent in the shops, leading to ever more growth. The unauthorised version: the tax cut would give an additional upward twist to land prices, creating an even greater crisis for those in debt – both home-owners and their banks. There can be no controversy about what did happen. In 2006, one year short of the peak in house prices (Graph 5.2), Bank of Ireland Private Banking published *The Wealth of the Nation: How Ireland's Wealthy Will Invest in the Next Decade*. It estimated residential property to be worth €573bn in 2005, and climbing. Within four years, the value of residential property had halved to €272bn.[3]

---

2 Pier Carlo Padoan (2014), Speech at the London launch of OECD *Forecasts During and After the Financial Crisis: A Post-Mortem*, February 11.
3 Building Industry Bulletin (2009), Dublin, p.2.

TABLE 5.1 **Irish Republic: farmland prices (€/acre)**	
2000	€4,860
2004	€6,480
2005	€15,400
2006	€23,900
2008	€21,000
2010	€10,500

The zealots did understand that capital gains were the name of the game. Farmland prices told the story: they more than quadrupled in just eight years (Table 5.1). Meanwhile, zombie governments were steering the economy with useless navigation tools. The implications were noted by the Irish Parliament's Joint Committee on Building Land when, back in 1985, it had warned that it could not compute the size of windfall gains from land. The Minister for Finance, it complained, could not provide precise information. The committee declared:

"It is unsatisfactory that the type of information necessary for assessing such an important policy area is not available."[4]

No action was taken on the recommendation to fill that information void.

The politicians could not claim ignorance. Ireland had been warned by Richard Crotty, a farmer turned lecturer at Trinity College, Dublin. He had an insider's view of the land market.[5] In 1981, in evidence to the Commission on Taxation, he explained that collection of the rents of land for the public purse would establish balanced growth and raise more than sufficient to enable the government to abolish income taxes.[6] He was ignored. Nothing, now, could prevent the emerging drama that Crotty had analysed in *Ireland in Crisis: A Study in Capitalist Colonial Underdevelopment* (1986).

From Backwater to Bankruptcy

In the 1970s, Ireland's GDP was 64% of the European Community average. Zealot politicians employed taxes that constrained the productive capacity of the population. People were penalised with the highest VAT, the highest income tax on the average worker and almost the highest excise duties and corporation tax on enterprises. But not everyone was suffering. In Dublin, land prices rose from €580,000 an acre in the mid-1990s to €8.6m per acre 10 years later.[7]

Between 2000 and 2006, house prices doubled relative to income and rents. About 15% of GNP was being generated from the construction of houses and

---

4 Irish Parliament, Joint Committee on Building Land, Dublin (1985), pp. xix, xi, 140.
5 Raymond Crotty (1980), *Cattle, Economics and Development*, Wallingford: Commonwealth Agricultural Bureaux.
6 Fred Harrison (1983) *The Power in the Land*, London: Shepheard-Walwyn, p. 208.
7 Frank McDonald and Kathy Sheridan (2008), *The Builders: How a Small Group of Property Developers Fuelled the Building Boom and Transformed Ireland*, Dublin: Penguin, pp. 7, 154.

TABLE 5.2 **Dublin: value of land in housing (€)**			
	1994	**2000**	**2006**
Average House Price	€72,732	€169,191	€305,637
Re-building Cost	€64,004	€121,818	€177,800
Land	€8,728	€47,373	€127,837
Number of Houses	26,863	49,812	88,219
Total Land Cost (€m)	€234.5m	€2,359.7m	€11,277.6m

Source: Building Industry Bulletin, Dublin, Sept. 2007, p. 19.

apartments – three times as much as in developed countries. In 1998, the year after the abolition of the property tax, the cost of land approached or exceeded construction costs. Rents rose 35%, and they were predicted to rise sharply in 1999 "due to a chronic shortage which, it is argued, should justify the restoration of Tax Relief for investment in new residential property".[8]

Assessments of the land market revealed a remarkable naivety. Eoin O'Cofaigh, the then President of the Royal Institute of Architects of Ireland (RIAI), claimed that "in theory at least, to say, double the number of houses per acre should significantly reduce unit land prices".[9] Output was increased, from 9,500 units in 1997 to more than 80,000 units in 2007. The cost of land did not decrease. It increased exponentially (Table 5.2).

Building companies complained that they were hindered by the planning system. And yet, according to Peter Bacon (who was commissioned by government to report on the state of the housing market), in Dublin the amount of land zoned for development was equal to eight years' worth of output at 1997 rates. Despite the availability of useable land, prices escalated. In the 10 years to 2007, the average price of a new home rose by 153%. Construction costs rose by 41%. The difference was captured in the price of land.

Rising "house" prices encouraged people to borrow more than they could afford so that they, too, could speculate in land-based assets. That gave further impetus to the upward twist in prices, creating the self-fulfilling prophesy that land prices would rise continuously. Ghost Towns appeared all over the country, quarantining the capital that could have been invested in cultural renewal. Instead, it was tied up in dwellings that many people could not afford.

Ireland was a nation humiliated. Taxpayers were forced to bail out the banks to the tune of €64bn. Finance minister Brian Lenihan (in an interview with the *Financial Times* on September 30, 2010), struck fear in the population by

8 RIAI (1998), *The Housing Crisis –Is Higher Density a Solution?* Conference Proceedings, Dublin, November 19, p. 46.
9 *Ibid.*, p. 6.

claiming that the collapse of the Anglo Irish Bank would "bring down" the whole country. People would have to bear the cost of keeping the corrupted financial sector afloat. Then the nation itself would have to be bailed out. International creditors laid out €67bn. The Age of Austerity exacted a terrible price on people who had played no part in the failures of governance. Eco-systems were wrecked and native species were replaced by ghost estates.

How did this culture of cheating take root in the Emerald Isle?

Formation of the culture of cheating

English adventurers arrived in the 13th century. They carved up the territory into private lordships. They were not interested in integrating themselves into the indigenous way of life of the Celtic tribes. The conquest and the transformation of the natives into tenants sealed the fate of the people. Historian Robin Frame summarised that colonial episode in these terms:

> "The institutions of English central and local administration were reproduced in Ireland; its law was English law, and there was to be no accommodation with Irish custom; the native Irish remained outside the official life of the colony."[10]

In the 16th century, more waves of settlers from England and Scotland intensified the process. Catholic-owned land was confiscated. Penal laws that restricted ownership to Protestants were promulgated. Those Acts were repealed in 1778. By then, the people were in no position to buy back their ancestral land. Now was the time to embed cost-effective techniques of social control. In 1831, Britain implemented the elementary secular education whose intent was summarised by historian Joseph Lee. The British sought to erase "subversive ancestral influence by inculcating in the pupils a proper reverence for the English connection, and proper deference for their social superiors".[11] Landless labourers were hounded out of the country: they included Nicholas Clooney from Windgap, Co Kilkenny, an ancestor of Hollywood actor George Clooney.[12]

Attempts were made to turn the cultural tide. During the Land War of 1879-82, the rebels declared that landlordism had to be "rooted out". Henry George reminded people of the process by which poverty was seeded under the guise of progress.

> "The introduction of the potato into Ireland was expected to improve the condition of the poorer classes, by increasing the difference between the wages they received and the cost of their living. The consequences that did ensue were a rise of rent and a lowering of wages, and, with the potato blight, the ravages of famine among a population that had already reduced its standard of comfort so low that the next step was starvation."[13]

---

10 Robin Frame (1977), "Power and society in the lordships of Ireland", *Past & Present*, No. 76, p.5.
11 Cited in G.O. Tuathaigh (1972), *Ireland Before the Famine, 1798-1848*, Dublin: Gill and Macmillan.
12 Jerome Reilly (2015), "George Clooney's kin were ruthlessly driven out of Ireland by neighbours", *Sunday Independent*, January 18.
13 Henry George (1879), *Progress and Poverty*, New York: Schalkenbach Foundation (1979), p. 306.

Henry George proposed that Ireland needed just one reform: a public pricing system that removed taxes from wages and profits and replaced the revenue with socially-created rent. His advice was rejected. Twice in 1882 while visiting Ireland on a speaking tour he was arrested as a trouble maker. The landed elites had learnt how to deal with challenges to their authority; going so far as to turn the land reform movement to their advantage (Box 5.1).

Box 5.1 **Nationalise or privatise?**

Michael Davitt formed the Land League in the 1880s. His condemnation of colonial culture was uncompromising: "The individualistic civilisation of the present system denies to the million the possibility of giving play to what is good in human nature, by putting its passions and selfishness into deadly activity in a cut-throat competition for wealth."* He wanted to nationalise the land. Everyone would be a co-owner. Davitt expressed a strong affinity for the philosophy articulated by Henry George, but he disagreed with the emphasis on fiscal reform.

Supporters of the Land League were offered a competing model of reform by Charles Stewart Parnell, a landlord and nationalist political leader who wanted the peasants to own the soil they tilled. His proposals were the least distasteful to the landlords in Westminster. When Protestant peers sought to diversify their portfolios, a Conservative government provided £5m as loans so that Catholic tenants could buy their land, with a further £33m allocated in 1891.

---

* M.M. O'Hara (1919), *Chief and Tribune Parnell and Davitt*, Dublin: Maunsel, p.250.

There was one prospect of redemption for Ireland. It came from an unlikely source – the Parliament in Westminster – when the Liberal Party achieved power with a mandate to reverse the course of history. The People's Budget was enacted in 1909 with the intention of shifting the State's revenue towards rents. Misinformation was one of the tactics of the opposition. In Ireland, the leader of the United Irish League, John Redmond, an MP who supported the Budget, defended tax reform in these terms:

"There is the most extraordinary misapprehension in certain quarters in Ireland with reference to what are called the land taxes...Take the case of the Lord De Vesci and Lord Pembroke, and the other wealthy ground landlords. Their land in the vicinity of Dublin a generation or two ago was worth no more than the ordinary agricultural land of the country. Since then they have not put sixpence into it by way of improvement; they have remained abroad, and left the land there. But the community by their rates [property tax], by the building of roads and streets, by the building of waterworks, the building of houses, the building of tramways, the laying of electric light, and so forth, have made this land in the neighbourhood of Dublin four, five, six and ten times the value that it was a couple of generations ago, and all that increased value is gained without the expenditure of one penny piece out of the pockets of these rich ground landlords. Well, now, this Budget proposes to put a tax on that increased value on these landlords, and I say it is a just tax." [14]

---

14 Budget League (1910), *The Budget The Land and The People*, 4th edn., London: Methuen pp. 91-92.

The Budget was not implemented. Nor would its spirit be carried over into Ireland with the declaration of independence in 1921. The Irish Parliament (Dáil) enacted the Land Act (1923) to complete the process of hooking farmers into the rent-seeking culture. The fate of the sovereign republic was sealed, as home-grown policy errors were driven by values that were an affront to freedom and justice.

The people of Ireland had fallen prey to the culture of greed. Absentee English landlords had drained the vitality from the island. The pattern – from warrior to banker – was the model that had worked in England. The people were bankrupted by aristocrats like Lord Downshire, who borrowed £186,500 between 1810 and 1840 without straining his credit worthiness. Landowners devoted a quarter of their rents to servicing debts. Some tested their creditors to the limits: the Earl of Lucan, whose estates were located in Mayo, had to earmark 85% of his rent to servicing his debts by 1905.[15]

Vales of tears

The most painful indicator of what happened to the people of Ireland may be termed The Case of the Missing Children. Their absence – over the centuries, numbering in the millions – bears silent witness to the corrupt character of the laws of the land.

Ireland had about 4m souls in 1780. The population grew to about 6.7m just after the Napoleonic war, reaching a little more than 8m in the 1840s. Through death and emigration, the numbers were reduced to 6.4m (1851) and 4.5m (1901). The population failed to recover during the years since independence. Almost a million people emigrated in the 1950s. The population was 4.6m in 2014. Systematically, the population was eviscerated to fit the cultural preferences of the lords of the land, both English and Irish.

In 2009 I visited the queues outside the soup kitchens of Dublin. Poverty could not (in the 19th century) and cannot (in the 21st century) be attributed to over-population. It was due exclusively to the culture of cheating (Box 5.2). Over 165,000 Irish aged 15-24 emigrated in the five years up to 2015, supplementing the 1m "active Irish passport holders" living abroad. Ireland endured significantly higher levels of emigration than any other country in the Eurozone. A rich and fertile land, fields crying out for the missing children, fields of tears that bear the footprints of rent-seeking speculators. In 2010, the government announced plans to introduce a certificate of Irish heritage for up to 70m people of Irish descent around the world who did not qualify for citizenship.

---

15 Michael J. Winstanley (1984), *Ireland and the Land Question 1800-1922*, London: Methuen., pp. 13-14.

> ## Box 5.2 **Land ownership and the exodus**
>
> When a global depression struck in the 1870s, Ireland was not able to cope because the net income continued to be siphoned out of the country. About 97% of the land was owned by men who rented it out to tenants. Just 302 proprietors (1.5% of the total) owned 33.7% of the land. Half the country was owned by 750 families.[1]
>
> Revisionist historians have sought to temper passions by suggesting that the landlord class was unfairly vilified. The number of dead or departed would appear to support the notion of a cultural cruelty. The injustices related to land ownership were seared into the collective consciousness of the people for good reason. An estimated 1.5m to 2m people died or migrated when blight struck their potato patches (1845-1849). Prior to the famine, migration was at an annual rate of 33,000 to North America, with a larger number heading for England. In 1841, the exodus exceeded 100,000.

1 Michael Winstanley (1984), *Ireland and the Land Question 1800-1922*, London: Methuen.p.11.

The tentacles of corruption

Corruption in the years of the Celtic Tiger penetrated deep into society, creating fortunes on the back of real estate ventures that fed tentacles into the real estate sectors in London, throughout Europe and across to the United States. The financial corruption of politicians and civil servants and go-betweens from the property industry was documented in two public enquiries presided over by judges Michael Moriarty and Alan Mahon.[16] Politicians gravitate naturally into the get-rich-quick syndrome that drives land speculation. Their hands are on the public purse strings, which makes them key players in the orchestration of networks with access to the easiest pickings – society's net income (Box 5.3).

One of the scene-setting acts was the cut in the tax on corporations. The decision was not driven by principle. The intent was to attract foreign firms that wanted to dodge taxation in their home jurisdictions. This was easier than the alternative strategy for creating jobs: tax reform that would foster home-grown enterprises to create sustainable employment in ways that conform to the disciplines of stewardship in community renewal and habitat conservation.

The European Union contributed to the flush-with-cash syndrome that encouraged many in civil society to get in on the act. When Ireland joined what was then the European Economic Community in 1973, it was classified as in need of financial aid. Far from viewing this as a national humiliation, subsidies from Brussels were treated by Dublin politicians as a right which they soaked up with delight. More than €60bn was poured into infrastructure like highways and railways. The productivity of the economy was raised, and the net gains were captured by the owners of land (this economic process is analysed in Chapter 7).

---

16 *Report of the Tribunal of Inquiry into Payments to Politicians and Related Matters* (Moriarty), Dublin, 2011; *Tribunal of Enquiry into Certain Planning Matters and Payments: Final Report* (Mahon), 2012, Dublin.

Box 5.3 **Pay-offs in the power-and-property network**

The *Sunday Independent* accused Fianna Fáil leader Charlie Haughey (who served in the top job of Taoiseach on three occasions) of perjury and stealing money. Haughey became an "egotistical kleptomaniac". Gene Kerrigan summarised the network around the politician in terms that define a corrupt society:

"He was part of a major white collar crime that involved large numbers of the well-off; business people, professionals, farmers, bankers and others. They used complex criminal schemes to defraud the state of hundreds of millions of pounds".[1]

Key events included a meeting in 1982 at which Haughey, in exchange for political support, agreed to sink money into inner-city regeneration in Dublin with tax breaks to lure private investors. But, the Financial Times correspondent noted, "the biggest winners were the builders and developers with the foresight to acquire large land banks before prices took off in 1994."[2]

1 Gene Kerrigan (2015), "It's now time to defend Charlie Haughey", *Sunday Independent*, January 18.
2 John Murray Brown (2008), "Lucre of the Irish", *Progress*, January, p.33.

The lists of shame are long, defining corruption and irresponsible behaviour in its moral, financial and institutional forms.

Among the politicians:

▶ **Liam Lawlor:** gaoled for his corrupt intervention in the planning system

▶ Ivor Callely: the gaoled senator who made fraudulent claims for expenses

▶ **Ray Burke:** former Minister of Justice who received back-handers of around £250,000

▶ **Francie O'Brien:** senator who attempted to extort €100,000 from a civil servant

▶ **Frederick Forsey:** Fine Gael councillor who accepted €80,000 from a property developer

▶ **Gwer Killally:** bankrupt county councillor who sought to cover debts by stealing

Among the institutions:

▶ **a police service** engulfed by scandals lost the confidence of the majority of people[17]

▶ **a civil servic**e that shelled out fortunes to "consultants", the money trail shrouded in secrecy[18]

▶ **charities** embroiled in scandals over the generous payments to their executives[19]

---

17 Maeve Sheehan (2014), "Poll shows 57% have lost some confidence in gardai", *Sunday Independent*, May 18.
18 Jody Corcoran (2014), "Cloaked in mystery: €165m spent in past three years is just the tip of the iceberg", *Sunday Independent*, March 9.
19 Joyce Fegan and Maeve Sheahan (2014), "Charities still reeling from aftershock of salary scandals", *Sunday Independent*, December 14.

▶ **a government** that compromised the parliamentary enquiry into the financial crisis[20]

▶ **the Department of Finance** which gagged the lone whistle-blower who tried to warn about the housing bubble[21]

Among the people:

▶ **farmers** welcomed the exemption from capital gains tax

▶ **bank regulators** suffered amnesia when questioned about the financial crisis

▶ **pop singers** continued to stash their wealth in foreign safe havens

▶ **home-owners** declared "can't-pay/won't-pay" the new water charge

▶ **fuel smugglers** pumped carcinogenic waste into the water supply[22]

The political turning point came in November 2014. As news came that the State had paid €33m over a deal involving a site worth less than €3m, opinion polls registered contempt for elected representatives. People turned out in the tens of thousands in towns across the country to express their anger. Government had lost the legitimacy that is contingent on the moral support of the population. The Celtic Tiger was now a Cowboy Cut-out. *Sunday Independent* columnist Gene Kerrigan optimistically suggested that "A new way of thinking is struggling to be born" (December 7, 2014).

The Pontius Pilate syndrome

The zealots want to cover their footprints.

Bertie Ahern, the Taoiseach (Prime Minister) who had presided over the abolition of the Residential Property Tax in 1997, confessed that the decision was a mistake. He blamed the "media and political pressure".[23] When warning voices were raised in 2007, Ahern wondered why the bearer of bad news "didn't commit suicide".[24] The €50,000 he had received while serving as finance minister in the 1990s was gifted from "long-standing friends" and were not corrupt payments for favours.[25]

John Bruton, the Taoiseach who presided at the launch of the 18-year business cycle in 1994, complained that the bankruptcy of the Irish Republic could be blamed on the European Central Bank, which he accused of a "major failure of supervision".[26] During Bruton's first year in office, Dublin held the presidency

---

20 Stephen Donnelly (2014), "Why I will not take part in this Banking Inquiry", *Sunday Independent*, June 15.

21 Daniel McConnell, (2014), "Woman who warned on house prices will be inquiry's star turn", *Sunday Independent*, July 20.

22 Jim Cusack (2015), "Provos dumping cancer-causing toxins into river", *Sunday Independent*, January 18.

23 Mary Regan (2010), "Ahern admits abolishing property tax was 'mistake' but blames media", *Irish Examiner*, May 10.

24 Ronald Quinlan (2014), "Bertie Breaks His Silence", *Sunday Independent*, November 23.

25 Owen Bowcott (2006), "Irish PM goes on TV to defend taking cash gifts from friends while finance minister", *The Guardian*, Sept. 27.

26 John Murray Brown (2011), "ECB Helped Fuel Irish Bubble, *Financial Times*, March 7.

of the EU which formulated the Stability and Growth Pact. That pact helped to wreck countries like Spain and Greece, as well as Ireland. Bruton has come to terms with his role in the débâcle, declaring that blaming bankers was "Almost like in the 17th century people blamed witches".[27]

Self-righteous zealots draw comfort from assurances that, at worst, guilt was shared. No one individual was to blame for misgovernance. Zombie political parties remain strapped in their ideological straightjackets, the lessons not learnt. Ireland remains a fiscal opportunist. In 2015, the UN warned that the privileged tax treatment it extended to corporations was injuring poorer countries.[28] Meanwhile...

▶ bankrupt property tycoons struggled to retain their homes as a new generation of speculators began to invest in the next wave of land deals

▶ the price of trophy homes in Dublin took off while a new movement of property owners opposed mortgage relief for victims of the previous boom

▶ corrupt lobbyist Frank Taylor left prison after 14 months, the proud possessor of a 1st class honours degree in Irish law

▶ the government decided to improve its revenue statistics by including citizens' earnings from prostitution and illegal drugs

▶ many owners refuse to pay the newly-introduced charge on residential property, while civil servants (to relieve stress levels) established a club to learn to crochet

There was a brief interlude when Ireland was astonished at the spectacle of principled politicians in their midst. The Green Party attempted to inject new thinking into policy. It advocated tax reform – in favour of treating rent as the public's revenue – when its six members were elected to the Dáil and joined a coalition government. They all lost their seats in the February 2011 election. Politically speaking, it was downhill all the way for Ireland. The culture of cheating had triumphed.

To acknowledge the fine work of the journalists of the *Sunday Independent* who diligently recorded the truth about Ireland during the period of my research, I will conclude with their assessment of the state of their homeland. The editorial published on December 21, 2014 warned: "Such, however, is the level of alienation today, we are moving towards the objective conditions required for the creation of a fascist state". A few days after that editorial was published editor Anne Harris's contract was not renewed.

---

27 Gene Kerrigan (2014), "We must default on health and welfare: Bruton", *Sunday Independent*, August 10.
28 Henry McDonald (2015), "Warning over Ireland's 'antisocial tax policies'", *The Guardian*, February 13.

Edmund Burke (1730–1797)

The integrity of a society is reflected in the character of the commons. Inter-generationally, people are linked by the gene pool from which they are drawn, the collective consciousness into which they are born, and through the moral codes to which the individual is sworn. Breaks in that continuously evolving drama can deform a culture, rendering it unfit to serve the authentic needs and wishes of the people. That is what happened to the Emerald Isle.

At some point in the malignant mutation of the anti-social virus in their midst, the people of Ireland would need to mobilise themselves around a prophetic voice. Around someone with the intellectual power to articulate a counter-culture. Someone graced with the charisma to drive awareness of injustice into the centre of political power, there to challenge the incumbent forces. Edmund Burke appeared destined for that role.

Instead, he became the voice of the landlords. They turned his words into the manifesto for conservatism, for the doctrine of leave-well-alone.

All the early signs had favoured the prospect that Burke could emerge as a champion for Ireland. The Burke family was victimised by the colonial land grab. Edmund was born into a Catholic family, the wrong side of the religious divide. He married a Catholic woman. His father had to convert to Protestantism so that he could work as a lawyer. The economics of apartheid had not only transformed the law of the land. Through its interventions in people's spiritual beliefs, it shredded the soul of the Celtic nation. To survive, over the generations people adapted their minds and behaviour to accommodate the alien culture.

Burke trained as a lawyer, and when he stepped off the boat in England he could have been expected to display a gritty determination to change the way of life back home. He was profoundly aware of the significance of heritage and its impact on personal and social wellbeing. In his most famous work, *Reflections on the Revolution in France*, he wrote that society was a partnership "between those who are living, those who are dead and those who are to be born". As a Member of Parliament, his advocacy would have resonated throughout the empire.

And yet, his reasoning on the human condition established his reputation as The First Conservative. His respect for tradition did not extend to sympathy for *the culture that might have been*, the way of life which people might have chosen if they were free from arbitrary constraint. His was a voice that preached against radical change. A voice that favoured tradition. Tradition created by, and for, those who bestowed upon themselves the title of Lords of the Land.

Burke was not a bad man but, ever so subtly, he was integrated into the English way of life. Two years after entering Parliament he purchased Gregories, a 600-acre estate near Beaconsfield – "a necessary part of the façade of a statesman"[29] – where he could formally entertain guests like the Duke of Portland.

Burke did raise his voice in opposition to crimes such as those in faraway India perpetrated by the East India Company. But closer to home, his fellow Irishmen needed someone who could forcefully explain to the British that the passage of time was not necessarily a good test of the virtues of custom and practice. By challenging the specious arguments employed by rent-seekers to preserve their privileges, he could have emancipated the authentic spirit of the people of Ireland, possibly freeing them to act in their best interests. We will never know what might have been, because Edmund Burke developed the doctrines which continue, to this day, to sanctify the politics of conservatism.

---

29 David Bromwich (2014), *The Intellectual Life of Edmund Burke*, Cambridge, MASS: Belknap Press, p.124.

6

The Killing Cult

THE KILLING starts at birth. Dispassionately and covertly. Even as the cells continue to be formed under the glare of light outside their mothers' wombs, a malevolent influence inflicts its deadly powers on the brains of new-born babies. The killing ends with the premature deaths of tens of thousands of people every year. People made to forfeit up to a dozen years of life, so that the culture of rent-seeking can flourish.

Killing with a purpose. Not random.

A pandemic if it came from a deadly virus incubated in Africa. A cradle to grave process.

What animates the culling of citizens in the richest nations on earth? Is the killing really infused by the ethos of a cult? In western democracies? Today?

Poverty is treated as a pathology that is largely attributable to the failings of the individual. It is, in fact, a pathology embedded in a population by a culture that breeds it as a by-product. The killing begins with the cells that constitute the limbic brain of new-born babies. That is the part of the brain that regulates emotions like love. By killing those cells, lives are affected forever. But poverty also has whole-life mortal effects. Pregnancies in areas with the highest levels of poverty in the UK are over 50% more likely to end in stillbirth or neonatal death.

Psychiatrists are now profiling the social environment of babies who suffer the attrition of brain cell development. Three of them write:

> "Recall that the brains of neglected children show neurons missing by the billions... As Winston Churchill observed, there is no finer investment for any community than putting milk into babies. The potential for humanity lives inside every infant, but healthy development is an effort, not a given. If we do not shelter that spark, guide and nurture it, then we not only lose the life within but we unleash later destruction on ourselves."[1]

---

1 Thomas Lewis, Fari Amini and Richard Lannon (2000), *A General Theory of Love*, New York: Vintage Books, p. 219.

Damage caused to the brains of babies exercises a lifetime impact. Researchers have correlated differences in academic test scores and family income to differences in the cortical thickness of parts of the brain regions.[2] Early genetic damage is also transmitted through the generations. Scientists at Cambridge University have confirmed that damage to genes caused by trauma or environmental stress can be inherited.[3] These factors can cause disease, premature ageing and early death.

The causal chain links the cells in the brains of babies to the public purse. To demystify the linkages, we need to begin by recognising the possibility that the health and welfare of a nation is ultimately determined by the way in which it uses rent. That flow of revenue is the source of society's vitality. The way in which it is distributed determines the character of communities. If people are not treated as equals in the disposition of rent, there must be a differential impact on the quality of their lives.

Historically, the killing began with the land grabs that displaced peasants from the commons. They lived in hamlets, their homes rudimentary but their environments healthy. They had the right to claim wood from the forests, to graze livestock on common land, to pick berries from hedgerows. Clean water came from streams. We should not romanticise their lifestyles. But life was healthy, given the level of development in the feudal era. Compared to the fate that would befall people in the 19th century, theirs was an idyllic existence.

As the land grab became a headlong rush in the 17th century, peasants were turned into vagabonds; dependent on Poor Law support in the 18th century, driven into the workhouses for the destitute in the 19th century. During those 300 years, families were ruptured, psychological health degraded, physiques depleted. Instead of leading ever longer lives, the legacy for the vanquished was shorter average lives. They were degraded by malnourishment and their social bonds were impoverished. Alcohol became a means of escape, ribald behaviour in ale houses the distraction for peasants vanquished from the cultural mainstream. The killing cult emerged as by osmosis as the rents of the kingdom were privatised. Life-giving cultural forces in the community haemorrhaged away. The change was reflected in the transformation of peasant recreational activities. In Saxon and Norman times, sports were "cheerless", such as bowling, fencing, wrestling.[4] Then, as change was violently imposed, people turned to bear- and badger-baiting, cock- and dog-fighting.

The account below is based on a summary of data culled from official reports and research by think-tanks which documented life in the UK in the years following the 2008 financial crisis.

---

2 http://newsoffice.mit.edu/2015/link-brain-to-anatomy-academic-achievement-family-income-0417 Accessed June 19, 2015.
3 Walfred Tang *et al.* (2015), "A unique gene regulatory network resets the human germline epigenome for development", *Cell*, 4 June.
4 Frederick W. Hackwood (1907), *Old English Sports*, London: T. Fisher Unwin.

▶ *Biological vulnerability* – stress induced as people were disconnected from the physical landscape by those who claimed exclusive ownership of land.

A government food report reveals that the poorest 10% of the population (6.4m people) consumed insufficient calories to maintain body weight. Children could not concentrate in school, and were attracted to high-energy, low nutritional value food (such as potato chips).

▶ *Psychological vulnerability* – stress as people were disorientated by the manipulation of values. Codes of behaviour were transformed to erase the moral right to share the rents that sustain the common good.

Suicide rates among young people hit record heights, with the highest rates in England's poorest region, the North-East. Data from the Office of National Statistics revealed a link between poverty and domestic abuse, with women in the poorest households more than three times more likely to be victims than those in higher income families.

▶ *Social stress* – endured as culture-scape was disfigured by the channelling of resources away from shared services. Funding favoured the culture that privileges the welfare of rent-seekers.

Self-harm among children aged between 10 and 14 soared by 45% in the four years to 2014. Children appealed to parents not to work so hard, and the Bishop of Durham declared that adults who chose to stay at home to look after their families were treated as if they were "not doing the best for the nation or the child". Almost half of employees surveyed did not take breaks from work, for fear that their bosses would think they were slacking. One *Financial Times*

Figure 6.1 **The Kill Zone**

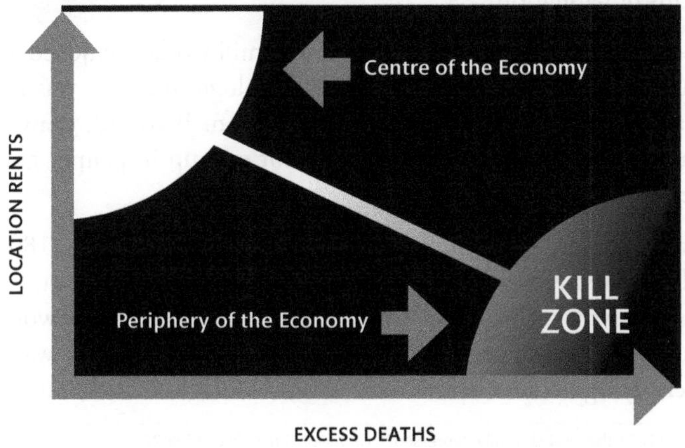

columnist, perceiving common threats throughout the west, asked: "Is the west clinically depressed?"[5]

Quests to explain premature deaths focus research at the micro level: at family breakdowns, the disintegration of personality, personal issues like obesity. These are symptoms of the pathology of rent privatisation. Surveys of micro behaviour explain the pockets of concentrated killing. The kill zones where death is visited on brain cells and human aspirations and on people who are about to retire are located at the margins of society where poverty is at its most intense (Figure 6.1).

From workhouse to welfare state

Marxists blame "capitalism", but the labouring people of Britain were victimised long before the arrival of mass production in factories. When the new forms of capital-intensive production were invented in the 19th century, the killer culture was already deeply embedded in people's lives. What happened in the industrial era helps to distinguish symptom from cause.

Factory owners had access to new sources of energy and a global market. Steam machines harnessed hydro power and fossil fuels. But human power was needed to load and steer the machines. The mill owners of Yorkshire scoured the workhouses around the country for the labour they needed.

▶ In 1844, the average life expectancy of mill workers in Bradford was 20 years and 3 months. An official enquiry into mortality rates in the hilltop village of Howarth – the home of the Brönte sisters – documented an average life expectancy of 16 years in 1870.

Premature deaths, beginning with new-born babies, were the products of over-crowded dwellings and human waste dumped in the midst of neighbourhoods. The deaths were intentional, in this sense. The net income produced by the working population – the rent – which ought to have been devoted to their collective welfare, was not spent on waste disposal, education, recreation and humane forms of habitation.

▶ A few miles away, in the village of Saltaire, mill workers enjoyed average lifespans of 70 years. Biologically and psychologically, there was nothing peculiar about them: they, too, had come from Bradford, drawn from workhouse populations. Why did they not end up in pauper graves in their early 20s?

The Saltaire workers were employees of mill owner Titus Salt (1803-1876). He decided to quit Bradford and relocate by the River Aire. He built a model village equipped with medical and educational facilities, places of worship, and homes with toilets. He was profit-centred, but he realised that there was no profit in his workers dying decades before their natural biological clocks ran down.

---

5 Edward Luce (2014), "Is the west clinically depressed?", *Financial Times*, December 22.

Nature cannot be blamed for lives cruelly foreshortened. It is the wilful intent of a culture that discriminates against segments of the population. Today, the postcode lottery continues to seal the fate of millions of people. Across England and Wales alone, an estimated 50,000 people die prematurely every year. That was the assessment of the late Dr George Miller. He was a member of the Senior Clinical Scientific Staff at Britain's Medical Research Council. He was also Professor of Epidemiology at the University of London Queen Mary and Westfield College. After reviewing the evidence, he concluded that the premature death of so many people in England and Wales could only be explained by tracing the mortal chain to its source: taxation, and the way fiscal policies affect the distribution of income, the production of wealth and the life chances of the population.

Dr Miller analysed Britain's social history and public policies in *On Fairness and Efficiency*.[6] His peers in the world of medicine, including advisors to the UK government (with whom he was on first name terms: they met at scientific symposia around the world), studiously ignored his findings. But there was no escaping the facts. Dr Miller's explanation for the deaths was based on a forensic examination of the impact of the public's finances on the health and wealth of the nation.[7]

The killing cult continued to operate into the 21st century, despite more than 60 years of medicine from the Welfare State. The pattern of the deaths emerges in the variations across the country. According to the privatised rent thesis, the highest number of foreshortened lives ought to be located in those areas where access to rents is at its weakest. I tested this hypothesis in *Ricardo's Law*.[8] By plotting death rates on a graph, we see a pattern which conforms to the profile of rent distributed across the economic space. People in the regions furthest from the centres of high net income endured a particularly savage deal in terms of life expectancy. I plotted the data on a straight line (following the old Roman road) north from London through Wallsend to Glasgow. Men in parts of Glasgow die, on average, 12 years earlier than their counterparts in the high-rent areas of London such as Kensington and Chelsea. Coincidence or the result of a causal mechanism? As the rents decline along the Roman road, we track a corresponding rise in premature deaths. The correlation cannot be explained in any terms other than the unequal share-out of society's life-giving rents in all its cultural, material and psychological manifestations.

The deadly secret of the highway tells us that Britain is founded on a set of laws and financial policies that pre-determine the life chances of each new generation. What is true of the profile of life expectancy across the country holds true for the prospects of babies within towns. In the greater Glasgow region, for example, the average life expectancy of males born in the low-income area of Drumchapel is

---

6 G.J. Miller (2000), *On Fairness and Efficiency: the Privatisation of the Public Income During the Past Millennium*, Bristol: Policy Press.
7 G.J. Miller (2006), *Dying for Justice*, London: Centre for Land Policy Studies.
8 Fred Harrison (2006), *Ricardo's Law: House Prices and the Great Tax Clawback Scam*, London: Shepheard-Walwyn.

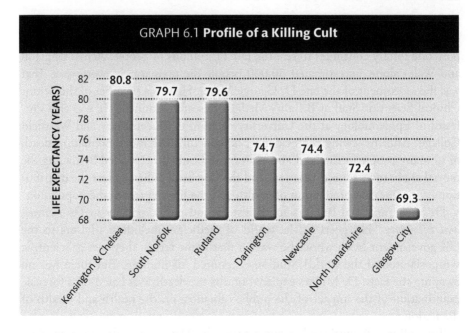

GRAPH 6.1 **Profile of a Killing Cult**

just under 70 years. In the adjoining neighbourhood of high-income East Dunbartonshire, average life expectancy exceeds 82 years. A difference of more than 12 years separates babies born out of the same gene pool who share the same health services. To attribute the difference to individual eccentricities is to shirk the ugly truth: there is something rotten in society that wrecks people's lives from birth. And spending more money on the National Health Service will not erase that death gap.

Harry Burns, the professor of global public health at Glasgow's University of Strathclyde and Scotland's former chief medical officer, insists that premature deaths cannot be blamed on individuals who succumb to alcohol or drugs or depression. He explains that

"people who don't feel in control of their life are stressed by it. Many studies have shown that the lower down a social hierarchy an individual is, the higher the levels of stress hormones in their blood. It appears that early childhood experiences can also produce lifelong abnormalities in the stress response. Stress is also associated with abnormal patterns of brain development in key areas...These are important for learning, decision-making, memory, stress regulation and emotional arousal."[9]

Prof Burns draws attention to the loss of industrial employment opportunities in Glasgow since the 1970s. This is not a sufficient explanation. Blackpool, which was never an industrial hot-spot, is one of the Kill Zones in England.

Some residents in the kill zones do live to ripe old ages, but they do so as *survivors*. Nicotine kills, a reality that is not controverted by the fact that some lifetime smokers survive to old age.

---

9 Harry Burns (2015), "Social failure, not lifestyle, has made Scots sick", *New Scientist*, January 26.

Killing the cultural hardware

Culture depends on the capacity of people to produce the wealth that sustains their lives and the commons which give them their humanity. The corrosive nature of constraints on production may be observed in every corner of our social galaxy.

The economy

▶ Growth over the past 200 years would have been far greater than the average of 2.5% which was achieved under the burden of the Treasury's favoured tax tools.

  – Taxes on wages raise the cost of hiring people. The fiscal burden renders low productivity workers unemployable.

  – Capital is misallocated. Investors seek "tax-efficient" vehicles rather than enterprises that maximise consumer satisfaction.

  – Land is sterilized. It pays to hoard sites while waiting for rents to rise even further, to generate greater capital gains.

The fabric of cities

▶ urban environments are damaged by taxes that hinder the organic evolution of communities and distribution of population.

  – Land speculation drives urban sprawl. Under-used inner-city land causes the overuse of peripheral locations.

  – Capital is depleted. Governments over-invest in highways and policing services to cope with scattered populations.

  – Social services are spread thinly. Schools and hospitals are delivered to sprawling outer areas at the expense of inner-city populations.

The natural environment

▶ Studies that estimate the cost of eco-cide fail to identify fiscal policies as responsibility for irresponsible behaviour.

  – Tax-funded incentives encourage over-use and depletion of finite resources. Natural habitats are impoverished.

  – Under-charging for the use of nature's services encourages pollution that exceeds nature's ability to absorb waste.

  – Aesthetic attributes of the landscape are eroded by cash incentives that subsidise farmers, who trample on natural habitats.

If governments comprehensively audited their policies to reveal how they kill the cultural hardware, the call for change would become irresistible. People would search for benign ways to manage the affairs of the nation. They would find answers buried deep in technical documents. The Institute for Fiscal Studies

(IFS), in its Green Budget 2015, notes that the "ideal long-term solution" to the problems of governance was to "tax land value irrespective of what, if anything, is built on it".[10] How many more avoidable deaths should be tolerated while awaiting the long term?

Killing the cultural software

No institution in Britain is immune from the organising principle which corrupts the commons into which babies are born and bred. By perverting an authentically human culture, the values that constitute our humanity are unglued.

The killing culture necessarily corrupts the institutions on which people rely for a healthy society. A book could be written on each of the issues listed below. We summarise them, and rely on others to provide the detailed documentation which is accessible through the public media. The randomly selected events that I spotlight cover the post-WWII years up to 2015.

▶ *Hacking telephones.* Newspapers are supposed to be the guardians of the public interest. Journalists were exposed for systematically breaking into people's private conversations to extract information. Employers paid heavily in legal costs and compensation to victims. Few reporters went to gaol.

▶ *Corruption of law-makers.* Members of Parliament falsified their expenses. When caught, a few went to prison, but the racketeering continued. The media reported that "dozens" of MPs rented out the nearby properties they owned while charging taxpayers the cost of renting homes or staying in hotels.

▶ *Health hazards in hospitals.* The revered National Health Services repeatedly exposed for killing by negligence or harming patients on a horrendous scale. Elderly patients, in particular, were vulnerable.

▶ *Law enforcement negligence.* Police forces throughout the country failed to meet their responsibilities. Public enquiries displayed institutional failures at disasters such as mass deaths in sporting arenas. The Independent Police Complaints Commission opened an investigation into Scotland Yard over claims that it covered up child sex abuse because of the involvement of MPs and police officers.

In the main, the people responsible for administering these institutions claimed they did not know their subordinates were breaking the law, behaving inhumanely or abusing people's rights. The plea of ignorance makes matters even worse. It confirms that the institutions are out of control, and that regulatory systems count for little.

---

10 *The IFS Green Budget* (2015), London: Institute for Fiscal Studies, p.288.

Tick-listing a sample of the sectors that have been corrupted by the culture of cheating needs to be set against the reminder that this could not have happened without cultivating in people the attitudes of irresponsibility. The integration of rent-seeking into the core of the collective consciousness had to surface as a generalised dissolution of public behaviour.

The sexual abuse of children

What began as the incestuous social inclinations of a relatively few narcissistic people turned, step by step, into the occupation of the cultural space that belonged to others. They colonised the collective consciousness, and thereby transformed the personality of the people. By their arrogance they claimed the authority to rule. Their credentials were fake, but they got away with it. One tragic indicator of their legacy – the dissolution of authentic humanitarian communities – was the tolerance shown towards sexual exploitation.

In 2008, when the banking seizure exposed the vacuum at the heart of the power structure, dark secrets began to ooze through the fissures in the system. Scandals revealed how institutions such as the BBC, schools and hospitals had been used by paedophiles on a shocking scale. For decades, the law enforcement agencies failed to fulfil their responsibilities towards the nation's vulnerable children.

By 2015, police records revealed an escalation in reported child sex crimes, which were increasing by 85 new offences every day. This was an increase of more than a third compared with 2014. The majority of victims were aged between 12 and 16, but more than a quarter of the cases – 8,282 – were younger than 11, according to the National Society for the Prevention of Cruelty to Children. Of those, 2,895 were estimated to be aged five or under.

The government was forced to set up an enquiry. The Chair, Sue Berelowitz, the Deputy Children's Commissioner for England, was not intentionally ironical in the way that she framed her warning – issued on May 30, 2015 – of what her investigation would reveal.

> "If the CPS [Crown Prosecution Service] were to prosecute everyone we would need a rolling prison programme. I would say there probably isn't the land to build enough prisons."[11]

Two days after that insight was shared with the public at the Hay book festival it emerged that her contract to chair the enquiry had been terminated by the Office of the Children's Commissioner (OCC).

What the landlords got away with doing to the whole population, perverts are doing to children.

---

11 Sarah Knapton (2015), "'Not enough cells' for child abusers", *Daily Telegraph*, May 30.

Dead money and the Dracula syndrome

If we attribute all of our problems to the failures of governance, we evade personal responsibilities. In truth, each new generation pays a heavy price for the irresponsibility of parents. The pathological state of the housing market registers that reality.

The normal behaviour for parents is to make sacrifices to create a better world for their children. But in the rent-seeking society, even the family is cannibalised. Natural history is reversed. Young people now not only pay high rents, many of them are also subsidising their parents through the taxes paid out of their wages. Those taxes fund the public services which their home-owning parents are using without paying the full cost of the benefits which they enjoy. We have a reasonably precise measure of those benefits, because parents capitalise the unfunded benefits into the value of the locations they own. In 2014, more people owned their homes mortgage-free than ever before. The English Housing Survey identified 7.4 million outright owners. In time, even the 6.9 million households with mortgages would accumulate debt-free capital gains.

The social cost of the good fortunes of home owners are measured by the increasing number of working households receiving housing benefit, to help them pay the rent.

▶ Housing benefits are capitalised into higher house prices. Private landlords made £177bn from rising house prices over the five years to 2014, ratcheting up the stresses that disqualify ever more young people from accessing the shelter they need.[12]

▶ Home-owners luxuriate in spacious amenities: half of them under-occupy their homes. Under-use of property is encouraged by property taxes that subsidise land-based assets. The costs are transferred to young people who are prevented from moving to find work. Immobility attributable to unaffordable accommodation constrains productivity.[13]

How the rent-seeking culture camouflages these dispiriting facts, converting them into good news, is disclosed in the way the housing crisis is represented. According to Shelter, the housing charity, young adults who cannot afford to buy homes "face decades paying out dead money to landlords". The psychological sub-text is that "getting on the property ladder" is the desirable goal. Outgoing rents are replaced by capital gains. But rent paid for the use of apartments or houses is *not* "dead money".

▶ People who built or funded dwellings with their labour are entitled to a return on their investment. The owner of a dwelling, if he offers the

---

12 *English Housing Survey Headline Report* (2015), London: Department for Communities and Local Government.
13 Kate Allen (2015), "Generation gap widens in housing market", *Financial Times*, February 26.

services of that building to others, is entitled to expect a reward from those who enjoy the benefit of the service rendered.

▶ The remaining part of rent, paid for the use of public amenities in a dwelling's catchment area, is not "dead money" either. If the tenants did not pay, taxes would have to be levied on the earnings of other people.

The anomaly in current arrangements is that the landlord, who does not provide the social services, captures part of the value which they create. That is the unjust part of the housing deal. That arrangement can be altered. Meanwhile, however, the "dead money" is the revenue collected out of people's earned incomes. Dead is the operative word.

If people declined, by democratic process, to pay the deadweight taxes, what would happen? Governments would have to revert to the direct collection of the value created by the services which are delivered to the public. Two things would happen. First, governments would balance their books. Second, the Dracula syndrome would be terminated. The cultural vampire survives on the life-blood of society. Starve it of rent and the killing cult would shrivel and die.

Anthony Charles Lynton Blair (1953-)

The theme tune as he strode in triumph into Downing Street was D:Ream's "Things Can Only Get Better".

They didn't.

As Prime Minister, Tony Blair promised to mobilise his New Labour party to unite the kingdom. People believed him, and gave him a remarkable legacy: three election victories in a row, beginning in 1997. Two decades after he walked out of Downing Street for the last time, the people of Britain were still trying to clean up the detritus of an economy that was guided, under Blair's premiership, to the worst crisis since the Depression of the 1930s.

In assessing Blair's record, we need to treat his words with caution. According to Jonathan Powell, who served as Blair's chief of staff for 13 years, "we apologised for things we were not responsible for" – such as Ireland's potato famine – but "we never apologised for things we had actually done".[14]

---

14 Jonathan Powell (2015), "Politicians who put on an act can expect little applause", *Financial Times*, February 13.

One of Blair's failures was the housing market. House prices peaked in 2007 – the year he resigned from Parliament. A year later, when investors realised that they held toxic financial instruments full of sub-prime mortgages, the banks seized up. Blair dissembled. "We didn't spot it. You could argue we should have, but we didn't."[15] There can be no controversy about whether he should have spotted it. I had given him a personal 10-year alert of what was going to happen. The response from Downing Street, dated February 23, 1998, was non-committal. "The Prime Minister has asked me to thank you for your recent letter and the enclosure." I followed up with public warnings, including the publication of *Boom Bust* in 2005. The information was in the public domain, but Blair's mind was closed. And his slick performance at the Despatch Box in the House of Commons helped to close the minds of others.

During his reign in Downing Street, the boom/bust property cycle was given free reign. Allied to the soft-touch approach to the financial sector, Blair presided over an administration that helped to fuel the land market to breaking point. But landed property and his tax policies were not held responsible for the social crisis that he nurtured. Instead, he blamed *capitalism*.

"Capitalism had driven the Industrial Revolution. Unregulated, unrestrained, untamed, its giant wheels rolled over the great mass of the people, squeezing work and profit out of them...for the benefit of the owners of capital."[16]

Under illusions popularised by Marxists, Blair interpreted the onset of democracy as the opportunity for the masses. Labour governments after World War II did attempt to amend the laws of the land, but they botched their chance. They applied socialist principles, so their tax policies and amendments to property rights could not be synchronised with the dynamics of the market economy. Consequently, their initiatives were struck off the statute book. Tony Blair could have learnt those lessons. He didn't. By his acts and omissions, he turned himself into one of the architects of the financial crisis. Today, he blames the financial sector as "the author of the wrong". Convenient, because the rent-seeking culture was to make Blair, the praetorian guard of the status quo, an exceedingly rich man.

After retiring from Parliament, Blair built a property empire. According to media reports, by 2015 his fortune was estimated at £60m. This included 10 houses scattered around England which he owned with his wife and three older children. That property empire was valued in excess of £25m.[17]

Blair diffused his wisdom widely, through lectures at Harvard and in his role as globe-trotting statesman. When the European Union began to split apart under the policies of austerity, he stepped in with advice. The pain endured by the people of Greece, he suggested, could be addressed by converging the interests

15 Blair (2011), *A Journey*, London: Arrow Books, p.667.
16 Blair (2011), p.213.
17 Luke Heighton (2015), "Houses dotted across the country and a £60m fortune", *Daily Telegraph*, June 13.

of all members of the EU. How? By deploying the fiscal and monetary policies which he had employed in Britain, along with "a clear, verifiable and enforceable programme of structural reform".[18] Those policies and reforms had widened the fissures in the disunited kingdom which Blair handed back to Queen Elizabeth when he went to Buckingham Palace to resign as premier.

---

18 Tony Blair (2015), "A grand bargain on Greece could be Europe's triumph", *Financial Times*, February 11.

7

The Con in Convergence

THE CLASS-RIDDEN kingdom would be united by the right to vote. That was the authorised doctrine that excited the campaign for universal suffrage in the 19th century. Today, some of us remain more equal than others, because politicians armed with the might of the state cannot overcome the forces that divide the United Kingdom. The electorate has grown weary of promises that are not converted into the freedoms that permit them to achieve their aspirations. The promise of convergence, of power trickling down to embrace everyone, is a con. But what was the confidence trick pulled on the people? And why can't they reverse the historic trends?

▶ *Convergence* rested on the "progress" that was promised by conservative philosophers in the 18th century. The gap between rich and poor would be closed and communities would be integrated to benefit from higher growth rates and a fairer share-out of the spoils.

▶ *Divergence* was the harsh reality. In frustration, utopian socialist projects were hatched, but the nation continued to be divided between Haves versus the Have-Nots, North *versus* South and, today, the Benefits *versus* the Bonus culture.

Someone, or something, exercised sufficient power to defeat the democratic mandate. Vast sums of taxpayers' money are still spent on trying to elevate the welfare of the socially deprived; to erase the deficits in housing, health and dignity. From the onset of the Welfare State after World War II to the crushing depression of the 2010s, governments struggled to keep up with the demands from people who wanted no more than a fair deal. But class division, economic havoc, political dissent and psychological dissonance remain as intense as ever.

Scholars who are paid to think about the Big Picture have failed to decode the malevolent dynamics behind the statistics. They lack a theory that makes sense of the evidence. Explanations are concocted, and new disciplines – like "behavioural economics" – have been invented. With a few exceptions, however, the experts maintain studious silence on the possibility that the one element common to all of the problems is the way in which the taxable capacity of the nation – its net income, or rent – is misused. Unravelling the Great Divergence is the first step towards solving the mystery, and that does not require the services of an Einstein. Two hundred years ago, the theory was spelt out by David Ricardo.

The analytical starting point is with the way people choose to apply their labour and capital to generate the most benefits for the least costs.

▶ Farmers gravitate to locations where fertility is highest and markets are closest. When the most suitable land is occupied they move to less advantageous locations, migrating outwards to the point where productivity is just sufficient to cover the costs of labour and capital. This location is the margin, at which point it is not possible to generate a net income: rent.

▶ The same principles shape the urban-industrial sector. Ricardo's model also applies to the way in which resources are distributed across a continent like North America or Europe. And, with globalisation, across the planet, as people seek to fulfil their needs as efficiently as possible, using the fewest inputs of labour and capital to achieve the best results.

Geoffrey West and his colleagues at the Santa Fe Institute, New Mexico, assembled data that exposed the unremitting logic of urban civilisation.[1] The statistics confirmed that labour and capital are deployed in locations where they deliver the highest gains. As Adam Smith had already observed, those private decisions automatically served the common good – *providing the correct pricing mechanism was used in the public sector*.

▶ **Declining costs** are achieved from increased capital investment in infrastructure. Large urban settlements require fewer resources to provide the services that people want. The bonus is delivered through the economies that are achieved by the scale of activity and investment.

There is an inverse relationship between size of settlement and the cost of services. One example: West measured the length of highways and found that bigger settlements needed fewer gas stations per mile. This means that public investment in infrastructure delivers a higher rate of return for private investors.

▶ **Increasing returns** are the reward for labour co-operation. Example: the denser the population, the greater the benefits from education. Universities in close proximity yield more innovations as knowledge expands at faster rates than the growth of urbanisation.

So why, then, is there so much deprivation in the largest, most efficient and innovative locations like London and New York? Is there an intrinsic weakness

---

1 Geoffrey West (2011), "Why Cities Keep Growing, Corporations and People Always Die, and Life Gets Faster", *Edge*, July 11.

in the market model, the whipping boy favoured by socialists? Was Adam Smith wrong to claim that people going about their private business would automatically serve the public good? Mass unemployment and the monumental waste of resources is an endemic feature of metropolitan life. In the UK, the human cost alone of the malfunctioning system is measured by the Office of National Statistics. Almost one third of the population – over 19m people – fell into poverty in at least one year during the years of the Coalition Government presided over by David Cameron. That figure was higher than the 25% average across the European Union and was only exceeded by Greece and Latvia.

The explanation for the pathologies that infect urban communities does not emerge out of the facts accumulated by Geoffrey West, who is a physicist. His work emphasises the aggregation of physical resources. He counted up the miles of gas lines, gas stations and the rest of the material fabric of urban civilisation to derive his insights on urban life. That was the hard and least fruitful way to decipher the dynamics of divergence eating away at the urban soul. Classical economists like Smith and Ricardo would monitor the trends by examining the urban economy's net income. Rents identify where the gains are located and who or what produces them. This analysis immediately exposes the raw sore in the system. The urban market economy is subverted by governments that employ dysfunctional tools for funding public services. Adam Smith's holistic model combined the Land Tax with the personal freedom to produce and consume. Without his Land Tax, the market cannot operate freely to deliver the optimum results.

Inefficient resource allocation

If we analyse the way in which prices are determined and incomes are distributed, we begin to perceive why the largest urban centres ("core" economies like London) grow into monstrous burdens. First, consider how the market economy helps people with their decisions on how, when and where to invest labour and capital.

▶ Competition equalises returns to labour. Higher wages attract people from lower wage areas until the rates are uniform across the economic space.

▶ Abnormally high rates of return to capital attract investors. Resources are rapidly reallocated, and profits are equalised to long-run average levels.

This appears reasonable: people are rewarded on a like-for-like basis, no matter where they live or work. But if this competitive ethos in the marketplace delivers fair outcomes in the labour and capital markets, where and why do things go wrong? As wages and profits are continuously equalised, there is a simultaneous response in the land market. Value is not *added* in that market. It serves as the sponge that soaks up the net gains produced in the labour and capital markets.

Box 7.1 **Charity for land owners**

In London at the beginning of the 20th century, low-income people were attracted to the borough of Southwark because Christ Church raised £350 a year to dole out bread to the poor. The competition for small houses, but especially for single rooms in tenement buildings, was so great that rents were considerably higher than in neighbouring districts. By this means, the clergy transferred £350 a year into the pockets of the owners of this kind of property, in the name of charity.*

A recent example of the sponge effect – financiers call it *arbitrage* – is provided by the tax concessions to investors who located in "enterprise zones". This experiment in charity was sponsored by Margaret Thatcher in the UK and President Ronald Reagan in the USA. The intent was the creation of jobs. Instead, owners of sites in the zones raised their rents to mop up the tax concessions. Investors could only balance their books by establishing labour-saving warehouse-type operations.

---

* Budget League (1910), *The Budget The Land and The People*, 4th edn., London: Methuen, p.99.

▶ Locations with the highest rents are the places that achieve the highest reductions in the costs of infrastructure and where the cooperative engagement of labour is at its most intense.

▶ The synergy from collaboration in the larger towns and cities is sucked up through competition for the sites that are fixed in supply.

It is not possible to make more land to meet demand in the City of London, so the demand for choice sites drives up rents. This sponge effect is a natural phenomenon, but the outcome need not be efficient or fair. All depends on how the public's revenue system is constructed (Box 7.1).

The *natural* tendency is to concentrate labour and capital resources in places and uses where they yield the most productive results. But a society that is dominated by the culture of self-serving greed, which is not regulated by the correct checks and balances, will ruthlessly concentrate rents (Marshall's *public value*) in locations where they can be most effectively appropriated. That is why the culture of cheating has to fashion a

▶ *hierarchical social system:* unequal power rests in the hands of those at the top of a class structure. They drain rents away from the bottom of the demographic pile; and a

▶ *horizontal spatial system:* predators concentrate power so that they can avariciously pull resources from the periphery into locations that become the social core.

The notions of "periphery" and "bottom" are *not* natural. They are artificial constructs designed to serve an unjust social system that is inhibited from distributing resources efficiently and fairly.

Figure 7.1 **Gravitational pull of resources**

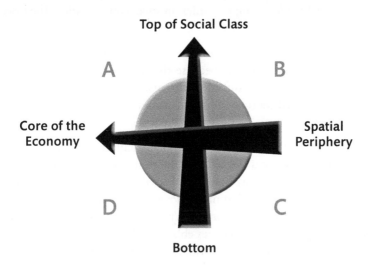

A balanced social system would create many more centres of excellence to achieve optimum outcomes. In that model, the production of material wealth serves both private needs while simultaneously enriching culture.

In the predator society, the dynamic thrusts operate at two distinct levels, the personal and the geographical. Vertically, resources are pulled from the bottom to the top, to enrich the individuals who capture the rents. Horizontally, resources are pulled to the central core, to impoverish the spatial periphery. These tensions are schematically illustrated in Figure 7.1, which charts the constant struggle over the distribution of power and rents. Most people want to combine efficiency with fairness in a balanced social system. Others seek to rig the rules so that they can cheat their way to riches. By following the flow of rent, we can infer key characteristics of the social system.

▶ If power and public value are channelled deep into quadrant A, society becomes monopolistic and people are regulated by a hegemonic ideology. Rents flow into the hands of a privileged minority whose political activities are framed to contain the discontent that infuses those at the bottom of the class structure.

▶ If society gravitates deep into quadrant C, anarchy prevails. Material resources and authority are dissipated. Society is directionless and communities are vulnerable to predators. Weak social solidarity renders people incapable of combining to generate the rents needed to fund growing, orderly communities.

▶ Gravitation deep into quadrant B implies the emergence of a feudal structure. In the absence of a comprehensive system of authority, people are vulnerable. This encourages them to seek the protection of Strong Men. Personal fiefdoms impose order on small communities. The price is paid in rents to the local Boss.

▶ Quadrant D suggests the most interesting possibilities. Gravitation deep into this field is not realistic, because that implies the centralisation of power combined with the diffusion of rents. The optimum formula is for rents to be collected centrally, and transparently, and shared with all levels of governance.

Human evolution is the story of the struggle to achieve a balance in the distribution of power and resources. Today, with the shift of the majority of the world's population into mega-cities, we have reached the point where the vitality of humanity is sinking into depletion mode. *Privately appropriated rents are causing urban centres to grow explosively, avariciously, wastefully.* Rural communities are marooned as their productive capacities ebb away. Young people are lured to the metropolis where they hope to find work, leaving behind ageing populations that slide into depression. What ought to be an enriching process – social solidarity through the efficient convergence of labour and capital – is undermined by the rent-seekers' pincer movement, which squeezes the life out of people and society.

The role of scapegoats

The skewed distribution of wealth and welfare is a nightmare for the intellectual and political elites. That is why they seek comfort in scapegoats. Who or what is to blame for the extreme stress caused by the disorderly growth of urban centres? Why, for example, are people being priced out of housing? It is agreed that, for many families, the construction industry does not deliver homes at affordable prices. Attributing the cause to the rent-seekers' nexus of Property Rights+Fiscal Policies is a no-no. So town planners – *bureaucrats!* – are scapegoated. They are a safe target, because under the terms of their employment as public sector employees they are sworn to silence. But dysfunctional urban settlements created by land owners pre-dated the onset of town planning by 200 years! By scapegoating the town planners, attention is distracted from the land owners who originally created, and continue to sustain, the political decision-making that distorts the urban economy.

The dynamics that create despair were evoked by the *Financial Times* in an editorial when it compared two ways of earning the same amount in London.

"The first is to work. A job in one of the capital's thriving industries will on average pay about £35,000. The second is to own enough office space for a few desks in the city's West End. Just 17 sq m currently yields about the same amount."[2]

---

2 *Financial Times* (2015), "The damage of London's artificial scarcity of land", May 20.

The *Financial Times* repeatedly analyses the incentives that put the power in the hands of land owners, among whom are the owners of residential property worth £1.5tn. Public debate, however, is continually misdirected by the lobbyists who are funded by rent-seekers. The purpose is to divide and rule, with the housing sector in the vanguard of that process. The way in which this then drives the divergence of society into Haves and Have-nots is illustrated in Table 7.1. This lists the average price of houses in the UK's four capital cities. London home owners enjoyed capital gains that were four times greater than Edinburgh's, and even greater than the other two cities. Even if (as shown in the last column) they all received the same increase over the period of one year equal to (say) Cardiff's 5%, the capital gain to London's home owners would be far greater. The gap would continue to widen over the property cycle, *even if the annual gain remained at a standard rate throughout the country.*

TABLE 7.1 **Divergence dynamics in the UK housing market**					
Capital cities	Average Price (£) April 2015	Price Rise 2007–2015 (%)	Annual price rise to April 2015 (%)	Capital Gain (£)	Capital Gain @ 5% (£)
London	422,700	35	11	46,497	21,135
Edinburgh	198,500	-5.8	5.9	11,711	9,925
Cardiff	177,400	0.4	5.1	9,047	8,870
Belfast	116,100	-49.1	6.0	7,002	5,805

Source: Hometrack UK Cities House Price Index (May 2015).

There is one answer only to the claim that planners are the problem. The market would deliver compact, people-centred urban environments if government *scrapped the planning laws and applied the efficient pricing mechanism to public sector services. That would terminate the hoarding of land, as all the rents would flow into the public purse.* But *that* would not be acceptable to the construction industry, which is primarily a land banking operation that builds houses to release the capital gains from their land.

The doctrine that convergence of life's opportunities is at the heart of the democratic process is a cruel deception. It is kept alive to con the vanquished into settling for crumbs, and the world of scholasticism is not about to change that prospect.

Paul Robin Krugman (1953–)

He has a great deal to say for himself on the subject of convergence in economics. Indeed, he presumes to preach to the public, and to instruct governments on how to go about their business. And people listen, given his status as a professor at Princeton and the recipient of the Nobel Prize for economics. What he has to say is of great importance. For according to the Nobel Committee, the prize was awarded to Paul Krugman for his work on the geographic concentration of wealth and the effects of economies of scale. These are exactly the issues that require the forensic attention of a world-class scientist, to help peripheral regions like Scotland. For communities suffer when their resources gravitate to core zones, at the expense of people who live in marginalised regions. Krugman has disseminated his knowledge in over 20 books, in over 200 scholarly articles in professional journals and through more than 750 columns in *The New York Times* and *Fortune* magazine. So when he was invited to talk about the concentration of wealth by the Institute for New Economic Thinking, he decided that he wanted to "do" land.

Speaking to his audience in New York, he referred to David Ricardo. But, alas, he had decided that Ricardo was of no help. Why? The English stockbroker turned economist had confined his analysis to agricultural land. Today, Krugman pointed out, Silicon Valley occupies land that was very fertile for growing fruit, but the location favoured the "agglomeration" that delivered economies of scale. This, he reported, was not something that would be found in Ricardo's *Principles of Political Economy*.[3] Not a promising start for someone who had decided to "do" land.

Ricardo did emphasise farmland in his theorising, but his description of how rent is formed encompassed the influences of both nature *and* society. In Chapter 2, On Rent, Ricardo draws attention to the "peculiar advantages of situation". For *situation*, he meant location. Some locations may be "less advantageously situated". Location. Location. Location. For farmers, awkwardly located farms implied (at the very least) higher transport costs for delivering produce to market; and higher transport costs diminish the net income, or rent. That is how rent becomes the interface between nature and society.

---

3 Paul Krugman (2014), speech, Institute for New Economic Thinking, New York, December 16; https://www.youtube.com/watch?v=RO8KWTb2iPM

Krugman's rejection of Ricardian rent theory, coming from a high-powered academic whose students accept his word as gospel, did not auger well for his analysis of resource convergence and income inequality. But Krugman appeared to redeem himself when he declared: "I love the idea that land should be a really important part of our stories". This was promising: if the professor from Princeton and Centenary Professor at the London School of Economics was willing to write "land" into the story that he taught his students, he would enrich macroeconomics. But as with all good scientists, he wanted to be "sure that this is really right". So he turned his forensic skills to the Flow of Funds accounts produced by the US Federal Reserve. This was his conclusion:

> "If we ask what the share of the net worth of household and non-profit sector was land, it was 8.4% [1975], it's now 10.6% [2013], which is not trivial, but not exactly overwhelming. It's not the kind of number that would support making land the core of your story about what is going on here. So either there is something wrong with the Flow of Funds numbers or this is actually not the direction you want to go. Which I am disappointed in because I love the story that says that values from land coming from agglomeration are an essential factor in the evolution of everything. But I don't really see it."

And that was it. The scientist flagged up the possibility of there being something wrong with the numbers, and then he walked away. What might have been a good "story" was left untold. Students sitting at the feet of the maestro were left blissfully unaware that the statistics on rent are treated in a disgraceful manner in US government records. That disgrace had been thoroughly exposed by Dr Michael Hudson, research professor of economics at University of Missouri, Kansas City, so there could be no excuse for Krugman's scholastic failure.[4]

Besides the methodological flaws that concealed the scale of the rent of residential land, Krugman chose to ignore the rents that are generated by industrial, commercial and other urban land uses; and by nature's services, which include the fortunes in rents being made from the

▶ radio spectrum
▶ wind power
▶ aircraft time slots
▶ nature's waste absorbing capacity
▶ salt water
▶ fresh water
▶ ...and a long list of other natural resources

Itemising the sources of existing rents, however, does not take into account the huge quantum of rents that would be generated if taxes did not suppress the creative energy of populations in every nation on earth.

---

4 Michael Hudson and Kris Feder (1997), *Real Estate and the Capital Gains Debate*, Levy Economics Institute, Working Paper No. 187 (March 1997); Michael Hudson (2002), "Lies of the Land: Illusions in US property appraisal methodologies", Geophilos 2(1); and *The Bubble and Beyond* (2012), Dresden: ISLET, Ch. 18.

Krugman's scholasticism is not the result of an idiosyncratic failure. It stems from systemic prejudice. The story of land had to be written out of the economic narrative.

The classical texts of Adam Smith, David Ricardo and John Stuart Mill were threats to the landed elite. At some point, economics had to be rewritten. This was accomplished at the turn into the 20th century by economists who debased their discipline. As substitutes for the flesh-and-blood realities of an economy constructed on the de-socialisation of rent, economists invented theoretical models based on fictions that delivered peace of mind to the rent-seekers.

▶ *People act rationally.* Private interests (taking current endowments as given) are best served by excluding government from the economy. Forget the public interest.

▶ *Markets are self-regulating.* Feedback mechanisms (such as the wisdom of the crowd) ensure stable equilibrium. Forget the cyclical propensity of the economy to implode.

Such doctrines successfully sanitised the culture of cheating by enshrining reality in a virtual cocoon. This was achieved by erasing the classical characteristics of "land" and "rent" from the language of economics. The guilty academicians are named by Mason Gaffney in *The Corruption of Economics*.[5] The linguistic manipulation was not intended to make economics more efficient as a solver of everyday problems. The evidence proves that. What became the school of post-classical economics failed to alert the world to the risks of the great boom in land speculation in the 1920s. This contributed to the policy shambles that led to the Great Depression of the 1930s (and the Great Depletion of the 2010s). It was as if the scientists at NASA, the American space agency, had tried to send men to the moon using a theoretical model which excluded the equation on gravity. If they had built their rockets with such impaired knowledge, take-offs from Cape Canaveral would have been spectacular for the wrong reasons!

The Guardians of our Minds continue to narrow the way we think. They exhaust us with spurious debating controversies between Left and Right, about Big Government versus Little Government, on the virtues of individualism compared to collectivism. This deflects attention from the reforms that would terminate the looting of the common wealth and restore the collective health of nations.

---

5 Mason Gaffney (1994), "Neo-classical Economics as a Stratagem against Henry George", in Mason Gaffney and Fred Harrison, *The Corruption of Economics*, London: Shepheard-Walwyn.

Part III

Outsmarting Evil

8

Lairds, Looters and Pots of Gold

THE PEOPLE OF SCOTLAND are angry. They know that there is something terribly wrong with the way their affairs of state are conducted. But in lashing out in frustration, they came dangerously close to making a terrible strategic mistake. By not recognising their enemy, they flirted with the idea of sovereign independence.

Sovereignty would have locked the Scots out of their share of a deep pool of riches – the pots of gold which they help to create. The looters in their midst would have breathed a sigh of relief...and the looting of Scotland would have continued unabated. Formal sovereignty, as the humiliated people of Greece have discovered, affords no protection against the brutal economics sanctioned by the culture of rent-seeking.

Fate saved the Scots. They are now free to fight another day. But as every good field marshal knows, victory belongs to the army that knows its enemy. So before adding up the spoils from a battle not yet fought, the Scots need to stare the opposition in the face. The opposing army's bayonets are drawn, and they are spoiling for a fight. To the death.

The people of Scotland were pillaged by three land grabs over the past 900 years. That process is not yet over. *The fourth Great Land Grab began on November 28, 2004.* Under the cover of an agenda called land reform, the rent-seekers launched what will become – if it is completed – the final triumph over Scotland. Aided by legislation that terminated feudalism, bankers are now milking the net income of Scotland – its rents – with impunity. The people, disabled by the most extreme concentration of land ownership in Europe, face an existential threat. At stake is their right to evolve an authentically people-centred culture.

The land grab of the 21st century fits the classic profile of the previous thefts: a culture programmed to kill people, gut humanity and consolidate a legacy of cheating. The common features are fivefold.

1. Control of territory to establish sovereign power on terms free of the duty of care to the working population

2. Extraction of public value to fund private privileges with the connivance of irresponsible political institutions

3. Amalgamation of farm land into larger estates and overseeing depopulation to maximise rents and minimise wages

4. Mobilisation of the flotsam population to expand the territorial domain through military action or colonisation

5. Concentration in urban ghettoes of the dispossessed population to manage civil distress and contain social costs

Understanding how the 4th Land Grab fits into this profile sets the challenge that now confronts Scotland. Can the Scots find the courage to break with the past and build a prosperous future? The alternative is to watch as their country recedes into the backwaters of the European Union, along with Greece and the other peripheral regions of the Eurozone.

The three historic events that bludgeoned the nation are documented by Andy Wightman in *The Poor Had No Lawyers*. He traces the evolution of authority from clan chiefs to the over-bearing lairds who looted the wealth so that, in due course, they could ingratiate themselves into the ranks of the English nobility.[1]

Land Grab No 1

▶ *Facilitated by warlords.* Feudalisation initiated by David I (1124-1153) spanned 300 years from the 12th century. Clan land was appropriated to reward foreign warriors who supported the Crown. Onset of feu duties (rents) payable for holding land.

Robert the Bruce (1306-29) was the warlord who developed the legal cover to give the appearance of legitimacy for the theft of clan lands.

Land Grab No 2

▶ *Facilitated by clergy.* Turmoil began in the 16th century with James IV and the occupation of church lands. The Catholic Church owned a quarter of the country, their land generating half the national land revenue. The clergy had become corrupted.

The occupation of church land was accelerated with the aid of venal priests who conspired with the nobility to secularise the sacred holdings.

Land Grab No 3

▶ *Facilitated by lawyers.* James VI (1566-1625) proclaimed the divine right of kings. The nobility feared their church lands might be reclaimed. They survived thanks to new laws which deemed a 40-year occupation of land sufficient to validate ownership.

1 Andy Wightman (2011), *The Poor Had No Lawyers*, Edinburgh: Birlinn.

And so Scotland became Europe's feudal bastion. The working population was required to pay feu duties to the nobility, an arrangement that remained in force until 2004. Its termination was heralded as a triumph: Scotland had finally modernised. In reality, it was the final nail in the coffin for the doctrine that the possession of land was anchored in social obligation.

Feudalism was constructed on the principle that social responsibilities were tied into the occupation of land. The feu duties were payments (in cash or kind) to the Crown. In time, these were hijacked by the nobility, who privatised the rents to fund narcissistic life-styles. But so long as feu duties were a social convention it was possible to argue that holding land was contingent on the obligation to fulfil a social role of one kind or another. Corrupted though that arrangement was, the concept of social obligation linked to land tenure would be important in one day liberating the powers of the people of Scotland. Instead, the formal abolition of feudalism consolidated the values of the rent-seeking culture. The land reform agenda that was originated by the Labour Party does not challenge the rent-seekers' demand that owners should be compensated by communities that wanted to liberate land from the lairds.

Land Grab No 4

▶ *Facilitated by bankers.* The price of land bears witness to the pathologies that distort people's lives. The accumulation of land into ever-larger estates is funded by banks, so that they can extract the rents as "interest" on mortgages.

The fourth land grab is monitored by Dr Duncan Pickard, a former university lecturer in animal physiology. He and his family farm in Fifeshire. The total area, owned, contracted and rented is 1720 acres. Because he purchased the home farm in 1992, when prices were in a trough, they were able to prosper. His land was valued at £4.5m in 2015. His land bank is the reason why bankers press him to buy more land; a proposal that he resists, because the numbers do not make sense. Based on the price of wheat, the rent of an arable acre was £85 (2015). So the sale price (at a multiple of 20 times the annual rent) ought to be £1,700. And yet, that acre sold for about £8,000. That was 4.7 times more expensive than its productive capacity, its economic use value, would warrant. That, in turn, prevented aspiring farmers from getting into agriculture. What drives the price to this insane level?

Land is not purchased for its economic value. The price reflects other considerations.

▶ *Quest for social status:* there is kudos associated with retreating from London to one's sporting estate to shoot deer.

▶ *Milking the taxpayer:* subsidies are handed out to help working farmers, but these are converted into land value.

▶ *Dodging the taxman*: free of inheritance tax and capital gains tax, farmland is "an efficient asset for the transfer of wealth".

▶ *A safe haven*: risk-averse foreign investors, in an uncertain world, seek security by investing their cash in land.

And so the price of land soars at the expense of local communities, which continue to be plagued by depopulation. In the 10 years to 2014, employment on Scottish farms declined from 63,832 to 59,636. People are driven into towns to subsist on tax-funded welfare benefits.

Family-sized farms continue to disappear as land is purchased for its investment value. Existing land owners who are free of mortgages are being actively courted by bankers to "borrow money" from them, to buy land they do not need. This exercise in milking the public purse is rewarding for the banks: it sluices the rents into their coffers (in the form of 4% "interest" on "loans"). The bait, for the owners of large farms who expand their holdings, is that they pocket the capital gains when they retire (or their children would, when they died).

This is the culture that the aristocracy wants to preserve, which is why it unleashed its attack dogs in Scotland. One of them has sharp teeth. William, the 4th Viscount Astor, wants to protect the Tarbert estate on the island of Jura. The 20,000 acres are held by a company registered in the Bahamas. The beneficiaries of that company are William Astor's three children.[2]

The Scottish government had declared its wish to support tenants who registered the wish to turn private land into community trusts. That mechanism would dilute the power of land lords. William Astor turned himself into a spearhead against the threat. He has friends in high places: he is the stepfather of Samantha, the wife of Prime Minister David Cameron. The Prime Minister had tasted the delights of the Scottish sporting estate, having shot stag on his wife's family's acres in the Hebrides.

Astor revealed his fury when he accused the SNP government of launching a "Mugabe-style land grab".[3] The reference to Zimbabwean president Robert Mugabe demonstrated that the nobility do not pull their punches. What had turned Mugabe into a villain? In 1979 he tried to negotiate the terms of a rational land reform when Britain agreed that Rhodesia could become independent of its colonial masters. Rhodesia's white farmers resisted, and a deal that was fair for everyone was not struck. Consequently, sovereign independence did not deliver prosperity for the majority of landless Zimbabweans whose ancestral lands had been grabbed by settlers from Britain. Mugabe turned violent.[4]

No Scottish politician was proposing anything that resembled a Mugabe-style land grab. The SNP had declared its wish to ensure that land was used for the benefit of the whole community. Nonetheless, it had to be intimidated – *just in case!* And so, the lairds launched a damage-limitation operation to re-advertise

---

2 http://www.andywightman.com/archives/3040
3 William Astor (2015), "The SNP land grab", *The Spectator*, May 23, p.16.
4 Fred Harrison (2010), *The Predator Culture*, London: Shepheard-Walwyn, pp.87-91.

their self-appointed roles as paternalists. They had their community's best interests at heart. But that was not how Dr Pickard saw it. From the conservatory of his farmhouse overlooking the rolling hills of Fife, he reflected on the way in which rural communities had been pillaged by the pathology of rent-seeking. In his view, the only land reform worthy of the name would start with the abolition of taxes on wages. Revenue, instead, would come from the rent of land. As a working farmer, he would be happy to place the rent of his land in the public purse. He would then be able to employ more people; instead of buying ever bigger tractors to displace ever more workers. But that is the reform that the rent-seekers really fear, which is why they had to unleash their attack dogs.

Keep what you create...

Restructuring the tax regime in ways that would deliver meaningful benefits for the whole population requires a new social contract. Could this be the historic mission of the people of Scotland? The new start would have, as its key financial principle: Keep what you create and pay for what you take. There is nothing extraordinary in that financial rule. It is applied in our daily dealings in the private sector. But who will offer leadership to the people?

The Scottish National Party (SNP) swept the board in the general election of 2015, capturing 56 of Scotland's 59 constituencies. Other political parties were wiped out. But electoral supremacy alone does not bestow the moral authority necessary to preach good behaviour. This is the SNP's dilemma. It lectures private enterprise on the "fairness" of paying employees a "living wage". At the same time, it enforces the rent-seekers' favourite taxes, which curtail people's freedom to earn a decent wage.

Restoring society's moral compass is an obligation on everyone. The opportunity for popular engagement in that challenge came when the SNP demanded

---

Box 8.1 **The gold standard**

Revenue raised directly from rent is the gold standard against which the damage caused by taxes must be judged. No damage is caused when revenue is collected from economic rent. In fact, rent-collecting policies are "better than neutral".[1] They positively support behaviour that increases wealth and welfare. This is how one economic textbook explains the point:

"Land will not be forced out of use, because land that is very unprofitable will command little rent and so pay little tax. Thus there will be no change in the supply of goods that are produced with the aid of land, and, since there is no change in supply, there can be no change in prices. *The tax cannot be passed to the consumers*".[2]

---

1 Nicolaus Tideman (1999), "Taxing Land is Better than Neutral: Land Taxes, Land Speculation and the Timing of Development," in Ken Wenzer (ed.), *Land-Value Taxation: The Equitable and Efficient Source of Public Finance*, Armonk, NY: M.E. Sharpe, 1999.
2 Lipsey, Richard G. (1979), *Positive Economics*, 5th edn., London: Weidenfeld and Nicolson, p.370. Emphasis in original.

"full fiscal autonomy". Would the people of Scotland insist on that power being used to eliminate the fiscal damage inflicted on them? They could choose to mandate a shift to benign ways of raising revenue. The public pricing mechanism that meets all economic and ethical tests has been called the Gold Standard method of raising revenue (Box 8.1).

In the transition to the full version of economic justice, what would happen (say) if the Scottish government zero-rated the income tax and replaced the revenue with a charge on the value created by the public's services? Forecasting the scale of the reward for that change depends on which measure of the damage inflicted by conventional taxes was used.

Mason Gaffney calculates deadweight losses using the average burden imposed by taxes. In his view – as perhaps the world's leading authority on the economics of taxation and real estate – the eventual gains from a rational reform of the public's finances would be much greater. His conservative ratio of 1:1 (£1 lost for every £1 collected) would deliver a much greater benefit than if we relied on HM Treasury's misleading estimate of the losses which it inflicts on the people of Britain (Box 8.2).

Box 8.2 **UK Treasury's misleading estimate**

HM Treasury admits that Britain loses wealth and welfare as a result of the way it collects revenue. Its estimates of the losses are not published by the Chancellor of the Exchequer in the annual budget he submits to Parliament. Using the Freedom of Information Act, I asked the Treasury to disclose such documents as they possessed which discussed how the income tax and the value added tax imposed burdens on people. The Treasury claimed that it possessed no such documentation. But they did acknowledge that they understood what is technically called the excess burden of taxation. Their measure of that burden was 30p for every £1 they raised.* That ratio of 0.3:1 is far lower than the estimates by academic economists. The Treasury estimate only includes the cost of collection and enforcing the tax laws. No allowance is made for the horrendous social, economic, psychological and ecological damage that governments inflict on the population.

---

* Fred Harrison (2006), *Wheels of Fortune*, IEA, pp. 30, 43-44, 155, 165, 173. The book is available free from http://www.iea.org.uk/publications/research/wheels-of-fortune

Table 8.1 identifies the losses, using Gaffney's 1:1 ratio. In 2014, the income tax raised £11.5 billion in Scotland. The loss of wealth and welfare to citizens was approximately equal to that sum. Between 2015 and 2021, the cumulative loss amounts to about £60 billion. This estimate assumes that the economy grows at an annual rate of 2%.

We do not have the numbers to fill in the end column: the number of people in Scotland whose lives are cruelly terminated – by up to 12 years – because of the fiscal regime.

The gains under an ethical financial arrangement would be greater still, if the UK government acceded to the wishes of the SNP and granted full fiscal

	Deadweight Loss (£ bn)	Cumulative Loss (£ bn)	Years-of-Life Lost (Proposed Index*)
		TABLE 8.1 **Losses to Scotland caused by the income tax**	
2015/16	11.50		?
2016/17	11.73	23.23	?
2017/18	11.96	35.19	?
2018/19	12.20	47.39	?
2010/21	12.44	59.83	?

* Defenders of the income tax must justify the annual role of premature deaths.

autonomy to Scotland. What would happen if regressive taxes such as VAT and National Insurance Contributions, which distort decisions on spending and investing, were abolished? Using those revenue policies, governments automatically create deep black holes – budget deficits which pile debt upon sovereign debt to burden future generations. The alternative strategy, basing revenue on rents, would *transform black holes into pots of gold*.

In 2014, the taxes levied in Scotland which damaged people's wealth and welfare added up to about £33bn. This calculation excludes those taxes that fall directly on rent (such as oil rents). Also excluded are the "sin taxes". If Scotland were free to abolish those damaging taxes and raised the revenue from rents, the net gain in wealth and welfare in just one year would be about £33bn.

But if the bad taxes were abolished, would there be sufficient rent to fund public services? The ATCOR thesis (see p.16) explains that *all taxes come out of rent*. This means that existing taxes are already derived from the nation's rents. The problems arise because they are collected *indirectly* and labelled "income" tax or "value added tax". By scrapping the indirect way of raising revenue, the "savings" would resurface as rents. The material reward for the reform is the bonus – the extra tens of billions of pounds a year – that would be shared between the private and public sectors.

Renewal through organic finance

The cornerstone of a successful community, whether a city, geographical region or on a continental scale, is the entitlement of everyone to share in the net income which they help to create. Within the UK, the people of Scotland contribute to the formation of the rents that surface in London and the high-rent south-east region of England. They are entitled to a share of those rents. It is called distributive justice.

The scale of the concentration of rents is illustrated in Graph 8.1 (the process of concentration was described in Ch. 7). The graph does not include commercial, industrial and other rent-generating assets, but it does provide a sense of the relative values. Rents slope down from London to Wallsend in the north-east of England, and then into Scotland.

Scotland contributes massively to the rents that surface in London. It shares its knowledge and its natural resources with London, sends its people to live in the capital along with personal savings for safe-keeping, and it is a market for London goods and services. On a *per capita* basis, Scotland contributes as much as Londoners to the UK's total net income. But because this is not understood, the kingdom is divided by a fractious squabble over the control of taxable income. The London-centric mass media and MPs claim that the capital delivers a "surplus" to the UK budget and that it subsidises Scotland and the regions. This is false accounting. Everyone in the UK economic space contributes to, and is entitled to an equal share of, those rents. Under a justice-based confederal structure, rents would be allocated on a *per capita* basis. There would be a significant transfer of rents from London and the South-East to Scotland and the other regions of the UK. Each region would be placed on an equal footing, and everyone would prosper.

The injustice of the present arrangement – the legacy of the lairds and lords – may be gauged by the human consequences of discrimination. London home owners are able to cash-in the imputed annual rent of residential land as discretionary spending. That income enables them to

▶ buy private education for children (enriching their lives)

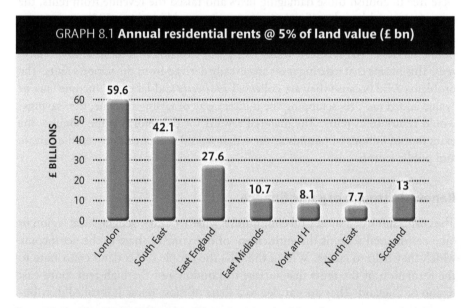

GRAPH 8.1 **Annual residential rents @ 5% of land value (£ bn)**

Source: Heather Wetzel (2014), *Welfare for the Rich*, London: Labour Land Campaign.

▶ trade up to more expensive homes (increasing their capital gains)

▶ supplement pension funds (luxury holidays during retirement)

▶ purchase luxury goods (all at a time of their choosing)

By sharing the net income, injustices of the tax regime – the economics of apartheid, of separate development – are abolished. Lifetime opportunities are equalised. At present, a significant part of Scotland's investible resources gravitate to south-east England. By changing the character of the public's revenue system, a balanced distribution of resources would be achieved to secure growth in all the regions. New synergy in the labour and capital markets would immediately surface in the building sector. Underused land in the most valuable locations would be brought into use. The increased supply of dwellings would level prices to what people could afford. This one short-term impact alone would do wonders in raising people's aspirations. Students sitting their final examinations would not need to have one eye on the prospect of jobs south of the border, and rural communities would begin to flourish, funded out of their own resources.

This is a holistic rehabilitation of society. Collectively, people are re-connected to their natural habitats and reintegrated into their communities. Personal well-being would be restored. The people of Scotland initiated the campaign for that programme of renewal to be turned into law at the beginning of the 20th century. They could do so again, today. If they were successful, they would lock all parts of the kingdom into a future of prosperity that could only get richer as the bonds of co-operation grew deeper. But to achieve this outcome, they will need to arm themselves with a meaningful definition of "sustainable development" (Box 8.3).

Box 8.3 **Lairds who live on charity**

Scotland's lairds celebrated when the Land Reform Bill was published in June 2015. The SNP government had publicised a "radical" approach to reform. Owners who obstructed "sustainable development" were threatened with being bought out. But lawyers gleefully noted that the concept of sustainable development was not defined in the proposed law.* This created the legal space for the lairds to argue that they *were* all about sustainable use of their estates.

The ultimate test of sustainability is a simple one: the ability to *pay your way*. To stand on your own feet. To meet social and environmental obligations. Scotland's estate owners fail that test. They are among the UK's biggest benefit claimants. They bank multi-million pound agricultural subsidies. They bank the rent subsidies received by their tenants from the taxpayer. They enjoy free use of public services. They convert nature's freely available energy sources into a stream of rental income. And they enjoy tax privileges when they bequeath their estates on death.

---

* Mure Dickie (2015), "Holyrood pushes for powers to force land sales", *Financial Times*, June 24.

The Right Honourable David Cameron (1966–)

We cannot accuse Her Majesty of being a liar, because the words she uttered in Parliament were written by David Cameron.

> "My government will legislate in the interests of everyone in our country. It will adopt a one nation approach, helping working people get on, supporting aspiration, giving new opportunities to the most disadvantaged and bringing different parts of our country together. My government will continue with its long-term plan to provide economic stability and security at every stage of life. They will continue the work of bringing the public finances under control and reducing the deficit, so Britain lives within its means. Measures will be introduced to raise the productive potential of the economy and increase living standards."

The speech, uttered on May 27, 2015, set the scene for yet another episode of parliamentary failure. The politicians believe their words; they may be sincere in their intentions, but they betray the expectations of the people. Cameron's words were crafted as the leader of the Conservative Party. The promises in the Queen's Speech were more or less the diametrical opposite of what would happen in the five years up to the General Election of 2020. The Queen's message was just another exercise in messing with people's minds.

An old English proverb asserts that "A man's house is his castle". A place of safety, shelter and privacy. The haven for one's family. That may have been true before the nobility turned their castles against the people in their hamlets. Today it is fiction. Residential property is a financial asset: the cutting edge of the quest for unearned fortunes. Politicians call it "getting on the property ladder". But they never talk about the collateral damage: economic apartheid, psychological trauma and social exploitation.

The apotheosis of the rent-seeking process was the savage marketing of sub-prime mortgages in the decade up to 2008. The outcome was the repossession of homes on a horrendous scale across the western world. Britain was at the epicentre of the culture of cheating. Democratically elected politicians like David Cameron do not understand the mechanics of this impoverishment. Otherwise, they would not be pushing people up a ladder which, for many, leads to hell.

Cameron is an honourable man. That's official. It's in his parliamentary title. So what do we make of this statement, which he uttered in his quest to persuade people to elect him back into Downing Street in 2015?

"Part of having a good life is having a home of your own. It's not about 'assets' and 'appreciating values' – it's about someone standing there with their keys in their hand thinking 'this place is mine.'"[5]

Why did Cameron deny that his plan was about putting capital gains in people's pockets? He wanted voters to believe that it was all about giving families security of tenure. He stressed this with his declaration that tenants in the social housing sector would be given the right to buy their homes. What lay behind the PR gloss?

On the day after Cameron's speech, one transaction that involved social housing made the headlines. The husband of Emily Thornberry, a Labour Member of Parliament, had purchased a housing association property for £572,000 in 2007. The mortgage was covered by the rent of the tenant, so did this mean there was no profit from the deal? In the intervening eight years the property's resale value was reported to have risen to almost £1m. But for Cameron, it was allegedly all about "security", not capital gains.[6]

The next Conservative Government will extend the Right to Buy to all housing association tenants in this country. That's 1.3 million extra families – a whole new generation given the security of a home.

That right to buy came with a golden handshake: a massive £100,000 subsidy transferred from the pockets of taxpayers, many of whom did not own residential real estate. But how could the purchase of the home enhance security, when social housing tenants enjoy security of tenure? The only good reason to take on a mortgage is to capture the capital gains that would accrue to the owner.

But it will get even better for folk on Cameron's housing ladder. He also promised them that, if re-elected, he would reduce the liability to Inheritance Tax. Again, it was people's homes that he had in mind.

"The home that you have worked and saved for belongs to you and your family. You should be able to pass it on to your children. And with the Conservatives, the taxman will not get his hands on it."[7]

Music to the ears of ageing citizens, the section of the electorate most likely to cast their votes in the election. But who would be the real winners? The Institute for Fiscal Studies calculated that the beneficiaries would be the owners of multi-million pound property, with no benefit for those who owned low-value homes.

▶ *"The home that you have worked and saved for belongs to you and your family."* No-one was challenging the ownership of residential property. What was at stake was the ownership of that slice of the value which Churchill called the "unearned increment". By the time a homeowner bequeaths the property, the sale price of the land beneath the dwelling would be about five times the value that could be attributed to the owner's labour.

---

5 http://www.politics.co.uk/comment-analysis/2015/04/14/david-cameron-manifesto-speech-in-full
6 Daniel Martin (2015), "Labour's Queen of Hypocrisy", *Daily Mail*, April 16.
7 Christopher Hope (2015), "Middle classes will escape the burden of inheritance tax", *Daily Telegraph*, April 13.

▶ *"You should be able to pass it on to your children."* No-one was challenging the right to bequeath property to children in the last will and testament. The forked tongue reasoning behind the Inheritance Tax bribe was coded assurance to property owners that they would not have to cash in their homes to defray the costs of care in old age. Those costs, instead, would be borne by taxpayers, and would fall disproportionately on people who did not own their homes.

▶ *"The taxman will not get his hands on it."* This is the nightmare of the land owner coming to the surface. The taxman has no interest in acquiring people's homes. His job (as directed by politicians like David Cameron) is to collect revenue to fund publicly-provided services. The issue in contention was the public value (rent), but David Cameron was not allowed to talk honestly about the nature of his party's bribes to the electorate.

The Big Lies came thick and fast. Cameron sought the return of a Conservative Government on the grounds that "We are on the brink of something special in our country". What was special about the next five years?

He claimed:

"We have drawn on all the resources of our nation to turn a great recession into a great recovery...We have put our country on *solid ground, laid solid foundations.* But let me tell you: the next five years are much, much more important...The next five years are about turning the good news in our economy into a good life for you and your family. Realising the potential of Britain...[the] country where a good life is there for everyone willing to work for it...a good job, a good home, a good start for your children, a good and secure retirement."

I claim:

In 2019 the Conservative government's "solid foundations" will buckle under a recession that will debilitate the "good life for everyone willing to work for it". Many people will lose their jobs, and the security of retirement will wither for even more people as the value of pensions are further eroded by political mis-management.

Middle-class home owners who work for their living are content with the culture of cheating. They are not evil people. They are trapped into doing wrong by the little white lies that weave webs of deceit and denial. Nonetheless, because of the onslaught of bad news, they are aware that there is a fundamental flaw somewhere in the way they are governed.

▶ *Young people* are forced to remain in parental homes because they cannot afford to rent their own homes. House prices will be inflated further by policies like the Conservative promise to subsidise First-time Buyers, as the sponge effect twists the price of dwellings ever higher.

▶ *Middle-aged* employees are locked out of the labour market. With productivity declining, Conservative financial incentives are biased in favour of labour-saving assets that generate rents. This adds a further downward twist in employment opportunities.

▶ *Elderly people* face the increased risk of destitution because Cameron's government changed the law so that pension pots (money saved on a tax-free basis, subsidised by low-income tenant-taxpayers) can be drawn down. Imprudent pensioners will have to rely on the Welfare State when the time comes to seek sanctuary in a care home.

The Institute for Fiscal Studies (IFS) calculated that Cameron's initiative on the Inheritance Tax would benefit 1% of home-owners – the richest in the land. But no-one computed the deadweight losses which were merely noted in passing by the IFS.

> "The undesirable distortions to savings behaviour and to work incentives have the potential to be significant...there is a danger that the tax proposals being put forward through this general election campaign will have a long-term malign influence on our tax system and economic welfare."[8]

The net effect of David Cameron's election promises in 2015 is to accelerate the rise in the price of land. His marketing pitch was a master class in how to transform the earned income of the working population into capital gains captured by those who own residential land. He was aided by his Chancellor of the Exchequer, George Osborne, who drove home the asinine mantra of the rent-seeking culture: "the basic human instinct [is] to provide for your children". Parents will sacrifice their lives to protect and provide for their offspring. But Cameron's Conservative Party consolidated a situation in which landed property is concentrated in favour of offspring who are already owners of residential property. Basic instincts are neutered for the majority to enhance the wealth of the minority.

---

8 Marion Dakers (2015), "Mansion tax relief plans 'damaging and malign'", *Daily Telegraph*, April 13.

9

The New Financial Architecture

DOROTHY Little is one of the rent-seekers' trump cards. Ageing and frail, she is the archetypal victim of heartless governments that threaten to ease the tax burden on working people. Cutting taxes is not the problem. *Replacing the revenue with direct charges on rent causes apoplexy*. People who live on Easy Street are ever alert to signs of threats to their privileges. And when threatened they do not hesitate to reach for their lobbyists, who publicise the sob story of the "poor old widow". How dare bully-boy reformers frighten old ladies with threats to deprive them of their meagre income?

Dorothy Little was coming up to her 70th birthday when she heard the news. The government intended to deprive her of the capital on which she depended for income. She was the stereotypical asset-rich/cash-poor widow. How could she survive? She set about manipulating emotions, as when she declared that "it is quite inconsistent with the character of the noble Englishman to reduce aged widows to beggary by forcibly taking their property from them".[1]

Mrs Little resided in Clifton, the exclusive hillside suburb of Bristol occupied by prosperous merchants who made their money out of tobacco.

And slaves.

Their homes were grand, and they hired servants to carry out the menial domestic tasks. Mrs Little's husband was long gone, and she relied on the cash flow from Jamaica to cover her living costs. And now the Wilberforce gang was pressuring government to emancipate the slaves!

But all was not lost. Mrs Little was championed by her son Simon, a barrister who brought his learning to bear on the Slave Compensation Board. Mrs Little wanted the price raised on the heads of the 13 men and women who toiled away in the heat of the Jamaican fields to keep her in comfort in her home in Bristol. In 1833, she was awarded £297 1s 6d for the job lot. She wanted £1,300. She placed £100 on the head of each of the men and women she owned. The commissioners were not moved by her appeals. So Simon deployed the sob story, warning

---

1 Hannah Young , "Dorothy Little – Slave Owner". Accessed May 10, 2015. http://britishlibrary.typepad.co.uk/untold-lives/2013/06/dorothy-little-slave-owner.html

the commissioners that they would "deprive[d] an aged widow of her property without any fault alleged on her part".

Parliament paid £20m (£16bn in today's values) as compensation to slave owners, 3,000 of whom lived in Britain. Mrs Little did not receive the price she wanted. She was furious. Parliament, she protested, had rigged the payments to favour those who owned land.

The ghost of Mrs Little now haunts Scotland, where the clarion call to land reform can be heard in the glens. The cash-poor widow was brought out of the closet when the Scottish National Party announced its commitment to land reform. The lairds want compensation. Their lobbyists, Scottish Land and Estates, commissioned research which showed that, depending on the scale of reform, landlords could require compensation of anything up to £1.9bn.[2] Furthermore, they suggested darkly, the threat to property rights contravened the European Convention of Human Rights. Viscount Astor protested:

"Are we really going to have to defend owning so many acres of hill when 500 acres of hill may be only worth the same or even less than one acre of good farmland in the lowlands of Scotland?"

Top price for one acre of wheat land sold for £8,000 in 2015. Would his lordship accept compensation of £320,000 for his family's 20,000-acre estate? This is less than the average price of two modest homes in Scotland. If put to the test, he would seek multiples of millions of pounds for the estate!

The correct fiscal approach to reform would not deprive Astor of any value which he, or his ancestors, had created. But now that the case for compensation has been raised by the landowners, it needs to be addressed. It opens up a hornet's nest for the lairds.

The first problem is to recognise the difference between slaves and land. Emancipation meant that slave owners would lose their "property". Erstwhile slaves would be free to depart and make their own way in life. Land owners, on the other hand, need not be deprived of their asset. All that should be required of them is that they (which includes those of us who own residential property) should play fair.

Under a rational form of governance, land owners cover that small extra cost incurred by the community in providing the services that each consumer wants to use. Those services are most efficiently valued by the value which each person assigns to the location he or she occupies. We conform to this pricing principle in our transactions in the private sector. In applying this pricing mechanism, the capital (selling) value of land would diminish to zero. But that capital value was not created by the owner. It is, in fact, a measure of the dereliction of duty on the part of government. The selling price of land (excluding the undepreciated improvements upon the land) is the rental value which government fails to collect.

---

2 Smiths Gore (2014), *Effect on values of extending succession and assignment to holdings subject to the Agricultural Holdings (Scotland) Act 1991*, London, p.36.

Land owners claim that the loss of capital value is an injustice: a "taking", as Americans put it. But the honest alternative way of viewing this outcome is this: *land owners are no longer subsidised by others, principally the tenant families who pay income taxes to government and rents to landlords.* During the carefully modulated transition to a rational system of funding

▶ values would adjust as the distortions caused by land speculation and status-seeking were eased out of the system. The rent of each location would reflect the value of available amenities, and would take into account the highest permitted use of land under planning laws. And

▶ deadweight taxes would be abolished. Land owners would retain all of the income they generated by going out to work or from their investments in capital improvements on the land (buildings, roads, fences). They would also enjoy psychic satisfaction of knowing that they were fulfilling their obligations to society.

But the compensation issue does not end with the land owner. We also have to consider the victims, and the compensation owed to them by land owners.

In 1833, Parliament conformed to its role as agent of the rent-seekers. It did not compensate the slaves. What was the cash-value of the pain caused by being violently dragged from one's homeland in Africa and being dumped on another continent, or an island on the other side of the ocean? What price for the high risk of loss of life in mid-Atlantic? For the humiliation of being auctioned on the quayside in Kingston, Jamaica? Of being shackled to someone else's land in perpetuity? Difficult though the exercise would be in estimating the price of all that pain, were those people not entitled to compensation? And shouldn't the compensation have been paid out of the rents which the slaves generated on the land owned by plantation owners?

In Scotland, should the lairds compensate the families whose ancestors were dispossessed? Clansmen scattered to the four winds after their cottages were razed to the ground by thugs hired by clan chiefs. Families who sought refuge in the slums of Edinburgh were exposed to the putrid conditions of overcrowding that caused many to die. Others, driven by desperation to migrate to foreign lands, faced hostile indigenous peoples. Should their offspring – like the families in the deprived districts of Glasgow whose lives are foreshortened by the culture of cheating – be compensated out of the fortunes accumulated by the lairds?

Re-living the pain of these episodes has its therapeutic value. Guilt and outrage have to be exorcised. Human rights were – and continue to be – abused. In reflecting on the horrors of past and present injustices, we come to realise the hopelessness associated with the idea of compensation for those who endured loss. Wounds need to be cured by concentrating on strategies which heal. A holistic approach is needed: assembling all the major cultural pieces into a healthy system that improves the welfare of us all. Re-starting social evolution with a Clean Slate.

Building trust by healing society

Altered lifestyles depend not just on people amending their personal habits (by exercising, eating habits, and so on), but also on the redesign of the cultural milieu. Re-socialising the nation's rents initiates a people-centred culture. Automatically, the moral compass is reconfigured as the laws of the land are rehabilitated. The economy would thrive like never before. The market (that is, people freely trading their labour and products *en masse*) would balance the principle of competition with a powerful sense of co-operation. Community rights would be aligned with the common-sense principles to which we already adhere in our private lives. The ethos of sharing would be viewed as complementary, not hostile, to private property. Populations would become self-conscious of the need to recover trust and stewardship as central to a strategy for outsmarting evil. In the course of nurturing these elements of a healthy society, the disgrace of the dozen years of life lost by many citizens would be transformed into a new lease of life.

But how can trust be institutionalised in a large and complex society? A new financial architecture empowers people to achieve their aspirations. This claim may be tested in relation to the concept of *money*, one of the adhesives at the interface between the public and private sides of our personalities.

Trust is built when we integrate into a harmonious single working system the pricing mechanisms which facilitate transactions between private individuals, and the transactions between each person and public services. This is the reality of the rent-sharing algorithm. To unwrap the algorithm, one attempt at its implementation is worth recalling. If enough people had understood the implications of what happened in the 1920s, the lives of tens of millions of people who died in World War II might have been saved.

Classical economists of the 18th century in France and Britain developed the knowledge which, if it had been applied, would have fostered a financial discipline grounded in responsible behaviour on the part of both nation-state and citizen. But in the 19th century, characters like George Warde Norman, the Bank of England director whom we met in Chapter 1, skewed the emerging institutions by submitting themselves to the mercy of the culture of cheating.

▶ If credit creation had been aligned with rent-based fiscal policy, Karl Marx would have remained an obscure romantic philosopher. Prosperity would have generated what the utilitarians in Britain called happiness.

▶ Instead, Europe endured two world wars because the governments of France and the UK wilfully refused to adopt the modernised Land Tax which was recommended by Adam Smith and his mentors, the French Physiocrats.

Our exercise in "what if" such-and-such had happened will motivate us to participate in the construction of a happier future.

After World War 1, hyperinflation destroyed the German economy. Elsewhere, the gold standard remained in place. The opportunity to chart a course away from mass unemployment occurred on New Year's Eve 1923. The German economist who was commissioned to solve the financial crisis arrived in London to meet the Governor who presided at the Bank of England, that all-powerful institution at the centre of the largest empire in history. When Wilhelm Ludwig Schacht stepped off the train at Liverpool Street Station he was greeted by the grandson of George Warde Norman. Their meeting would turn out to have momentous implications. *The mission on which Montague Norman and Wilhelm Schacht were about to embark could have laid the foundations for a prosperity which might have diverted Europe away from the madness of Adolf Hitler.* The formula for peace and prosperity was contained in the financial algorithm which Schacht had been ordered to create in Germany.

The plan was to establish a parallel currency and anchor it to the rent of German land. The Deutschmark had become worthless (a barrow load of notes was required to buy a loaf of bread!). The Rentenmark would exist alongside it. The government would issue a mortgage on all agricultural and industrial property, with an annual levy set at 5%. The prospects for Germany were limitless. For example, by raising revenue from the economy's net income (instead of taxing wages and profits), the State would liberate the creative energy of the German people. At the same time, the State would become financially solvent. The need to pump out worthless Deutschmarks would disappear. People would invest and produce in the confident knowledge that the value of their output would not be eroded by inflation or taxation. *This was the financial algorithm for happiness that Montague Norman's grandfather, George Warde Norman, had kept a secret from the people of Britain.* It was now placed in the lap of his grandson for implementation at a time of crisis that threatened the future of Europe.

Montague Norman was not impressed. His grandfather was one of the architects of the doctrine that credit needed to be backed by gold. Not the rent of land. But he did work with Schacht, and the Rentenmark came into being. It had the desired effect. Inflation was brought under control. But once the value of the Deutschmark was stabilised, *the Rentenmark project was terminated.*

Valuable lessons were learnt as a result of this experiment. If Norman had shared his insights with policy-makers in London and Washington, those governments would at least have had the option of forestalling the land boom that was beginning to take off in the UK and the USA. Instead, encouraged by the biases in the tax regime, the land speculators who drove the boom/bust cycle in the 1920s were free to wreak their cyclical havoc. Speculation in real estate in hot spots like Florida drove global stock markets into the frenzy that culminated in the Crash of 1929.[3]

The Depression of the 1930s was an Act of State. The knowledge that came out of Germany could have laid the foundations for prosperity unparalleled in

---

3 Fred Harrison (1983), *The Power in the Land*, London: Shepheard-Walwyn, Chs. 5-9.

history. Social psychology would have been transformed, not least in Germany, leaving no political space to be occupied by the sociopath Adolf Hitler. Europe might have been spared the slaughter in the trenches, homes bombed to smithereens, millions gassed to death in concentration camps.

This exercise in counterfactual history enables us to think about the forks in the road of life. The future is not pre-determined. We have choices. These include, of course, travelling down dead-ends.

Making money

The role of bankers and their bonuses in the making of the 2008 crisis aroused anger in many people who now focus their reforming zeal too narrowly on altering the status of money. They propose that the power over credit creation should be transferred to government. But far from building trust from within the financial system, that banker-bashing plan would open up dangerous terrain.

Recall that the bulk of the revenue captured by banks from the value-adding economy is rent (Chapter 3). The rents are appropriated either directly (mortgages), or indirectly (such as providing the finance for rent-generating infrastructure). But the alternative proposed by critics of the money system is also imperfect. They want money to be made available by (say) an independent Money Creation Commission (MCC). It would decide how much money to create and government would decide how to spend it; in doing so, pumping the money into circulation.[4] Furthermore, they want that money to be made available "interest-free".

This would be jumping from the financial frying pan into the financial furnace. Instead of every person participating in the production of wealth and welfare, and in doing so, determining the quantum of credit in circulation as required by their activity, we would have the Wise Men of the MCC. They would consult the statistics and decide whether to allow the money supply to expand or contract. Something similar happens today. Central bankers consult their runes and pontificate on desirable levels of macro-economic activity through their forecasts of such indices as the rate of inflation or the rates at which various forms of "money" circulate in the economy. Those statistics range from poor to dangerously useless.[5] The methodologies of statisticians, guided by post-classical economic ideology, predetermine the results. Their models appear to make sense while the going is good in the economy; but they retreat in humiliation when the real economy departs from the narrative authorised by the numbers. Iceland is contemplating the adoption of sovereign money (Box 9.1). Its prospects may be gauged by looking at what happened in the American state of North Dakota when the fracking industry came to town.

---

4 Andrew Jackson and Ben Dyson (2012), *Modernising Money*, London: Positive Money.
5 Sarah O'Connor (2015), "Office for National Statistics under fire over data errors", *Financial Times*, June 1.

Box 9.1 **Banking on sovereign money**

Iceland was bankrupted by its banks in 2008 because economists and managerial financial experts did not know what they were doing. They allowed the money supply to fuel real estate prices to breaking point, and engaged in trades in financial instruments that were loaded with "toxic" mortgages. Why should they be any more reliable if they were given the power to create the country's money supply? As the Financial Times observed:

"Sovereign money may force banks and their shareholders to think harder about the loans they issue, but does not on its own dispel the spectre of speculative excess".*

Speculation would inevitably continue, because rents would still be slushing around in the system. The availability of "interest-free" money would intensify the land-driven business cycle, which would be no blessing for anyone except the current owners of land.

* *Financial Times* (2015), "Iceland's daring raid on fractional reserve banks", April 10.

The Bank of North Dakota is a public bank. Its record is impeccable in supporting both a network of small community banks and the State government's public agencies.[6] But what happened with the advent of fracking?

Median house prices in the US peaked in 2006. Then, throughout America, the average price of residential property collapsed from $200,000 to a low of $142,000 in 2009. House prices in North Dakota went in the reverse direction. They rose from $125,000 to $141,000. By 2014, the rate of increase in house prices in North Dakota eclipsed the rest of America, reaching $195,000. In some hot spot counties, home prices were roughly double the median US price. In Williston, prices more than quadrupled. Why? *Oil rents*. New technology made it possible to extract petroleum from shale. Wages were high, as the industry attracted workers from around America; but the cream off the top of the bonanza was soaked away by the land market. The fact that a publicly-owned bank anchored the State's financial affairs did not prevent land owners capturing a large slice of the oil rents.

There was no immediate negative impact on the North Dakota economy, because of the price competitiveness of shale oil on world markets. But if the Dakota effect had happened on an economy-wide scale the outcome would have been a property boom/bust with the power to destroy jobs and cost many people their homes. And that is what would happen if a public agency created "interest-free" money. The "interest" that was previously charged by banks would not remain in the pockets of Labour or in the profits of Capital. It would be soaked up in the market for Land, offering no relief to families who struggle to pay rent or the mortgage.

The solution is to integrate the credit and fiscal systems as narrated by James

---

6 Scott Baker (2015), *America is Not Broke*, San Francisco: Tayen Lane Publishing.

Robertson, a British proponent of that synthesis.[7] In a society in which State and citizen honoured their respective responsibilities, money would cease to be a menace. If rent was paid into the public purse, there would be nothing for bankers – or any other rent-seekers – to pocket. The creation of credit would be determined by the needs of people engaged in value-adding activity, as was explained in Chapter 3. The risk of an authoritarian government taking control of the nation's money would be avoided.

Alvin Rabushka (1940–)

The existential conflict between feudal nobility and folk of the commons had to be fought through a struggle to control the institutions of the State. Commanding the heights of parliamentary power gives the victors control over the public purse.

It was an unequal contest. The rent-seekers won. But the guardians of the culture of cheating can never drop their guard. Complacency would be particularly dangerous in a democracy, which nominally empowers even the vanquished. One cost-efficient strategy for perpetuating privileged power is to nurture grievances against government. This can be achieved by manipulating language to corrode trust in public finance. Enter the doctrine of the Flat Tax.

Dr Alvin Rabushka preaches the Flat Tax from the citadels of academia. He is a Senior Fellow at the Hoover Institution at Stanford University, California. Less conspicuously, he disseminates his doctrines as a member of the libertarian Mont Pelerin Society.

Rabushka's flat tax has been adopted by former communist states across Europe and Asia. Nearly 300m people in post-Soviet Europe live in flat tax regimes. His agenda is readily shared with the mass media. He readily advertises his attitude towards government: "Starve the government, fire the bureaucrats. Fire the bureaucrats, starve the government. Let the government go hungry for a while".[8] He publishes a list of more than 40 countries which he claims have implemented

---

7 James Robertson (2012), *Future Money*, Cambridge: Green Books; Joseph Huber and James Robertson (n.d.), *Creating New Money*, London: New Economics Foundation.
8 Interview, SAST Report, http://sastreport.x10.mx/ra.html (Accessed June 2, 2015).

the flat tax (http://flattaxes.blogspot.co.uk/). The poignant economy on that list is Hong Kong.

From where did Rabushka get his doctrine of the flat tax? In 1973 he travelled to Hong Kong to conduct exhaustive interviews with officials who administered the British colony. He was impressed by the honesty of the civil servants, their diligence in treating everyone fairly and efficiently, and the remarkably low taxes levied on the residents of this island outpost of the British Empire. He documented "the peculiarities of Hong Kong's anomalous practice of public finance" in a book which defined *anomaly* as "adherence to the concept of balanced budgets".[9] With virtually no economic aid from Britain, the colony succeeded in providing world-class public services while balancing its budget. Remarkable! How did *bureaucrats* accomplish this feat? Rabushka did not disclose the secret in *Value for Money*. He managed to skate over the one significant peculiarity about the British colony.

He did, however, manage to misrepresent Hong Kong's financial history. He noted that Britain took possession of the island in 1841 and "did little more than maintain law and order and raise taxes to pay for the cost of the civil establishment and necessary public works". That artful summary failed to alert readers to a unique financial settlement for the colony. The Foreign Office in London prescribed an alternative way to raise revenue. Because the territory was acquired from the Chinese government on lease, it had to be rented out to users.[10] Consequently, the costs of administration were defrayed by the rents that merchants were happy to pay to locate their businesses on the island. *Rents are not taxes.* Unless, of course, one wishes to alter the meaning of words and to declare that America's corporate landlords are in the business of collecting "taxes" from their tenants.

When Rabushka visited Hong Kong in the 1970s, a large part of public spending was funded out of the rents generated by public infrastructure. This financial architecture made it possible to keep taxes low. The deadweight on the population, therefore, was also low. And so the productivity of Labour and Capital was very high.

Rabushka broadcast the good news about what he called a unique kind of governance on his return to the United States. He failed to highlight the significant role played by land. But it was that land-and-rent arrangement which made it possible for capitalists to coin their profits while conducting their business on leasehold property. That little detail would have disturbed Rabushka's doctrine of property rights and public finance.

In 1981, Rabushka began to preach the virtues of a simple tax regime. What he did not tell his audiences was that, by keeping taxes low, income would be transferred to land owners in the form of higher rents. That would have interested

---

9 Alvin Rabushka (1976), *Value for Money: The Hong Kong Budgetary Process*, Stanford: Hoover Institution Press, p.1.
10 Fred Harrison (1998), *The Losses of Nations*, London: Othila Press, p.ix.

the people of Eastern Europe in the post-Soviet era. Footloose rents would automatically gravitate into the pockets of the emerging class of oligarchs. That value would then be redirected into the purchase of high-value real estate in Western capitals rather than invested in value-adding enterprises in countries like Bosnia and Herzegovina.

Wouldn't the erstwhile communists have benefited if their governments had separated the profits earned by Capital from the revenue attributable to Land? Rabushka had his answer ready:

"[I]t is difficult to separate the value of land from the value of the buildings on it".[11]

Without that separation, it is not possible to treat the public value as a unique source of revenue for funding public services. The valuation exercise did not defeat Britain's civil servants in Hong Kong (Box 9.2). Nor does it defeat the property speculators who know exactly how to value land apart from the undepreciated capital improvements on the land.

Box 9.2 **Hong Kong: the state as ground landlord**

In writing about the wealth of America, Alvin Rabushka noted that the Hong Kong government "does not adhere dogmatically to a *laissez-faire* style of management in all of its public activities. The state is the ground landlord in Hong Kong and spends between 15 and 20 percent of the national income providing roads, compulsory primary education, extensive medical and health services, subventions for numerous social welfare agencies, and public housing for about half of the population...Since low-income households pay no income tax, rising incomes translate into more purchasing power and a higher standard of living. Thus the free-market system (*sic*) appears to be effective in bringing about rapid economic growth and a more even distribution of income, without any need for government-directed, tax-based redistribution schemes".*

* Alvin Rabushka (1985), *From Adam Smith to the Wealth of America*, New Brunswick: Transaction Books, p.146.

The flat tax doctrine did not make headway in the West. Nonetheless, it continues to be used as an ideological tool to foster hostility towards government. That technique is employed to ferocious effect by the London lobbyists who have taken the name of Adam Smith in vain.

Every year, the Adam Smith Institute announces Tax Freedom Day. This is "the day when Britons stop working to pay their taxes and start earning for themselves". In 2015 that date was May 31. The institute deploys this device to insidiously cultivate the idea that, while working to pay their taxes, people are "working for the government". Not themselves. Subliminally, this encourages the thought that government is separate from – even hostile towards – the people. That public finance is somehow unconnected to the personal interests of those who pay taxes.

---

11 Robert E. Hall and Alvin Rabushka (2007), *The Flat Tax*, 2nd edn., Stanford: Hoover Institution Press, p.167.

The honest narrative would be to note that, out of 365 days in the year, it took 150 days to fund the services that people wanted to purchase via their government, and 215 days to fund the services that could be purchased from private suppliers. But that formulation would not serve the ideological purpose behind the corruption of the collective consciousness: divide and rule. The Director of the Adam Smith Institute, Dr Eamonn Butler, does not pull his punches:

"The Treasury hates Tax Freedom Day, because they don't want us to know how much tax we really pay...Mediaeval serfs had to work about a third of their time for their feudal lord, but we are in serfdom to the government for even longer!"[12]

There are defects in the tax regime, but good governance is not fostered when minds are coloured by language which conceals the inner realities. So it is not surprising that, in championing the Flat Tax, the Adam Smith Institute overlooks the virtues of rent-as-public-revenue. It does draw attention to the deadweight losses suffered by Labour and Capital. But it declines to raise awareness of the most efficient revenue raiser.

The Institute is also silent on the macro-economic impact of the Flat Tax. The flat tax "should put the national economy in a much more secure position within the lifetime of one Parliament".[13] If the Adam Smith Institute's favoured flat tax had been introduced in 2015, even more of the nation's rents would have been transferred into the land-led housing cycle's date with the next property crash. Adam Smith, who enshrined the Land Tax at the heart of his canons of good taxation, would have been horrified at the way his name is taken in vain.

12 http://www.adamsmith.org/blog/tax-spending/today-is-tax-freedom-day-2/ Accessed June 3, 2015.
13 Richard Teather (2005), A flat tax for the UK, London: Adam Smith Institute Briefing, p.5.

10

A Unified Theory of Humanity

HUMANITY is at stake. After the terrible deeds of the 20th century, no-one can contest that claim. We now have the technology to wipe out our species, in the way that we are doing to other life-forms on planet Earth. The practical challenge that we face is painfully simple. Those who shape public opinion, who monopolise the public platforms of communication, are unable to explain how we can escape from the traps that have been set by the alien culture which dominates our lives.

I have offered a theory which explains how we can rescue humanity. By applying its principles, we can release ourselves from the grip of the culture that is cheating us, a culture that prevents us from realising the full potential that is latent in our selves. The theory accounts for why early humans combined their innate ingenuity with the resources of nature to generate a unique flow of energy. That quantum of value emerged out of the synthesis of human labour with the energy of nature. Our ancestors had the wisdom to invest that energy in the formation of a new realm of existence in the universe. The social galaxy is a human creation which takes its place alongside the natural galaxies that constitute the universe.

The social galaxy is a fragile invention. A simple arithmetical relationship reveals the inner beauty of that creation, and of the harmony of the relationships between nature and human species. I will illustrate this with its financial manifestation.

Of all the value that we labour to create, half of it is rent. What Alfred Marshall called *public value* is rent reserved to fund the spheres of our existence that we share in common. This is how the numbers add up.

▶ The average tax-take is about 35% of national income. This is rent mislabelled as taxes on "income" and consumption. The amount of rent that remains in public hands is approximately 17% to 22%. We may safely assume that 50% of national income is rent. I call this the *sacred* income because it sustains those activities that define humanity.

▶ About 50% of production is divided between wages and profits. This is the profane, or secular, flow of energy that sustains us biologically; providing the material means for procreating the species through time, sustaining the activities that enable us to glimpse that there is more to life than the bare necessities.

Thus does the financial algorithm reveal a perfectly balanced symmetry. The 50/50 harmony secures a balanced relationship between the private and public sectors in the material world. And, in relation to personality, it secures balance between private self and social life. By fusing the two layers – the material world with our personal lives – optimum conditions are created for dynamic interaction. That dynamism created, and now sustains, the social galaxy.

Thus, we see that the future of the social galaxy depends on the integrity of every person who claims to be a member of the human race. Abolishing the culture of cheating, which is now the most important challenge facing our species, is a personally disturbing prospect. The obligation on each of us to pay for what we consume represents transformation on a revolutionary scale; and that arouses anxiety. And yet, the pricing mechanism which would deliver that transformation is so self-evidently correct that it arouses confusion. It is contrary to what we have been schooled into believing. For a start, don't we already pay for what we consume? And anyway, aren't public services so different that we cannot apply a pricing mechanism based on the same principles that apply when we buy groceries?

The upheaval is, in the main, psychological. There would be no dramatically visible ruptures to the way people go about their daily business. That is what makes this a quintessentially British (as opposed to French, Russian or Chinese) revolution. Incremental adjustments, sympathetically executed over a manageable timescale. Reassuringly modest changes to institutions while empowering everyone to work and play as never before.

The objective is steady-state progress. Freedom to create the life of one's choice while contributing to the common good. Those contributions could be either material (working to add further value to the wealth of the nation) or spiritual (engaging in social or artistic ways to add to the health of the population).

It is not my job (or anyone else's) to prescribe the detail of the way of life that would emerge further down this road. Future generations would be free to choose how they wished to arrange their affairs. Our obligation is to define the elemental rules of justice, and to demonstrate how they can be enacted to launch society on a new age of enlightenment. But we do have to specify ways of facilitating the transition. In practical terms, how can the financial algorithm be synchronised to work with the grain of our frail human condition? How can it erase the psychotic nature of the culture that infuses our lives and pervades our communities?

We avoid utopia-speak by reminding ourselves that rent-seeking stems from a natural inclination. It is based on the desire to fulfil our basic needs with the least possible exertion. That is the stimulus which animates curiosity, and in turn results in the innovations that increase our productivity. Creative energy leads to more fruits produced on the back of less labour. Thanks to the genius of our ancestors, a formula was developed ("the market") that made it possible for them to measure and share the benefits of those innovations. That enrichment of the public space accelerated the pace of social evolution. To sustain our humanity we have to find a way back to that path of innovation, because that is the only way to accumulate the resources needed to fund the next evolutionary stride into the future. So we will now consider how to work our way out of two awkward legacies bequeathed to us by rent-seeking. How do we recover our public spaces? How do we reassert our credentials as custodians of good governance?

Stewardship of public spaces

In walking through open spaces in London, in places like Canary Wharf or the King's Road, Chelsea, being challenged by private security guards comes as a shock. Aren't these public spaces? No, they are not. The men in uniform are there to remind us that open spaces in the midst of shopping malls or office blocks are owned by private corporations. We may traverse the spaces with their permission.

The alienation of public space is a symptom of the rent-seeking agenda. Governments that deprive themselves of the rents they need, trap themselves into authorising urban renewal by privatising yet more of the public domain. Cash-strapped governments increasingly rely on private corporations to provide social infrastructure. This irresponsible arrangement arises solely because of the failure to employ a robust revenue system. The budget deficit is funded by the public in general: social assets – such as public spaces – are yielded to private investors. Recovering the social status of those open spaces is one test of the capacity of people to serve as stewards of the common good.

Globally, we have reached the point at which more people live in cities than in rural areas. Demographic concentration will create enormous problems in the 21st century, but the solution cannot be based on Mao's model – forcibly relocating people back in the countryside. So how can we rebalance people and public space organically, without the use of violence?

Draconian measures, such as the nationalisation of corporate property, are not compatible with the need to democratise society. The organic approach would be to require the corporations to pay into the public purse every penny of the rents that are attributable to those spaces. *Open spaces used by the public enhance the attractions of shopping malls and commercial properties.* Corporations, accordingly, raise the rents paid by their tenants. Those rents are not created by corporate landlords; they are created by, and belong to, the public who make the locations valuable.

Charging the full rent of those locations (while simultaneously cutting taxes on wages and profits) automatically engages people and private corporations in a new ethos of responsibility towards each other. They become joint stewards of the public space. That renegotiates their relationship as participants in a value-adding process. The benefits are maximised. Everyone wins. Stewardship would emerge out of a democratised financial process.

▶ Rents would be recorded in publicly accessible registers, so that citizens may audit the value of their presence and their activities.

▶ Owners and users would be accountable for their behaviour: good behaviour raises the rents that fund the shared public services.

Some corporations may choose to relinquish the responsibilities associated with ownership. That would be for them to decide. But handing back ownership to the public would not reduce the locational value that benefits their adjoining properties. Rents would continue to flow into the public purse.

Custodianship and Good Governance

One of the corrosive consequences of the tax burdens imposed on people is political apathy and antipathy towards politicians. The moral challenge is to gather the strength to reassert our collective rights and responsibilities as the custodians of good governance. But what does that entail?

The character of political power is determined by the relationship between the citizen and the State. The State holds the whip hand, today, for one reason only: it controls the public purse. That purse is replenished with the power to enforce intrusive taxes. That is an unequal relationship, but balance can be restored if people reclaim their power. There is one practical way only to achieve this: asserting the power of the financial algorithm. Rent-as-public-revenue. This formula empowers people to decide

▶ what services they want from the State
▶ how much they will pay, and
▶ when they will pay

By basing government revenue on rent, decision-making is transferred to the people in a way which conforms to the organisational complexities of urban society.

The rent-based formula permits people to pay for the services they want, as determined by their personal decisions on where to live and work. The choice of location rests with the individual, who knows the cash value of the services that are accessed at each location (estate agents leave them in no doubt!). No-one is forced to make those choices. The individual decides whether to occupy a high-value or low-value location, based on personal preferences. That is the first step towards serving notice to the State that a people-centred politics has become the order of the day.

▶ Rents are *voluntary payments into the public purse.* They are not arbitrarily fixed by government according to the level of one's wages or consumption preferences.

▶ Payments are tailored to the consumption of public services. In return, government has a duty of care to the public, and must use the rents to maximise the population's welfare.

By exercising the democratic right to determine their financial arrangements, people establish the terms of a new kind of governance. People are empowered, and notice is served to the State that a people-centred politics has become the order of the day. By this means, people convert themselves into custodians of governance. By their choices, beginning with the resources they freely decide to place in the public purse, they frame the terms under which policy-makers may operate. The will of the people prevails in the most practical of ways, by regulating *how revenue is raised, how much is raised and how it is spent.*

Funding the new social contract

The renewal of the humanitarian project is just the beginning. Once unleashed, the pots of gold begin to flow.

In fiscal year 2014-15, the British government was forecast to raise £565bn from taxpayers.[1] That was not the total cost of taxes. We must add the losses that accrue as a result of the way government raises its revenue. In offering estimates of those losses, we do not seek spurious precision. The numbers cannot be exact, but that should not prevent national treasuries from issuing health warnings: their taxes are bad for people's health and welfare. Tobacco companies are required to issue such health warnings on their packets of cigarettes. Similar warnings issued by national treasuries would quickly prompt people to re-engage with politics.

Table 10.1 illustrates what would happen if the UK Treasury raised its revenue directly from net income. GDP would have been much bigger! How much bigger depends on which measure is used to account for the losses. To calculate the losses, the revenue from taxes that fall mainly on rent, such as the local property

TABLE 10.1 **UK bonanza from financial reform (2014–15: £ billions)**			
Revenue raised by using Deadweight Taxes (author's estimate)	*Income gained by eliminating deadweight losses*		
	UK Treasury's ratio (0.3:1)	**Mason Gaffney's ratio (1:1)**	**Others (2:1)**
565	+170	+565	+1,130

---

1 HM Treasury (2015), *Budget Report*, House of Commons HC 1093, p.6.

tax, is excluded. Also excluded are the "sin" taxes that people may wish to retain for health reasons (on alcohol and tobacco).

▶ The minimum gains, using the UK Treasury's estimate, are excessively low. Under this measure, the *additional value* to be shared between government and the people would be about £170bn. The maximum gain, using the ratio favoured by some economists (£2 lost for every £1 in tax revenue),[2] would be £1,130bn.

▶ The conservative measure of gains is based on the ratio advocated by Mason Gaffney. His ratio of 1:1 suggests that if the UK raised its revenue directly from rent, the gain would be of the order of £565bn.

GDP in 2015 was estimated at £1.8 trillion. Add in the gain that would accrue under the new financial algorithm, and GDP would have been at least £2.3 trillion. That is a fabulous additional increase in wealth and welfare, to be split 50/50 between the public and private sectors; between the private life and social self.

A democratised financial system would accept the obligation to account for the potential output that is being denied to the population. The rent-seeking culture camouflages the losses to the public at large by fostering delusions. In the UK, for example, the Treasury includes in its annual Budget report to Parliament a section entitled "Fairness". The 2015 report insists that "the richest households will make the biggest contribution to reducing the deficit both in cash terms and as a proportion of their income". The Treasury fails to add that those rich households would claw back from the public value much more than they paid in as a result of the way the rigged fiscal rules elevate and distribute capital gains in the housing market.

Citizen's rent dividend

Responsible governance cannot be achieved without corresponding responsibility on each and every citizen. Rights must be anchored in equivalent responsibilities for both the citizen and the State. This poses a moral dilemma for a population that resolves to adopt the rent-as-public-revenue algorithm. One immediate consequence, as we have seen, would be an increase in the income. The temptation would be to treat the State's share as a surplus which could be divided between all citizens (even rich folk) as a dividend. The proposal of a basic income that was distributed unconditionally to everyone, *viewed in isolation*, is not tenable on either moral or practical grounds.

The concept of a Citizen's Dividend is advocated by many social reformers as a means to ameliorate present economic hardships and injustices. It would not do so, for two reasons.

---

2 Martin Feldstein (1999), "Tax Avoidance and the Deadweight Loss of Income Tax", *Review of Economics and Statistics*, Vol. 81(4), p.678.

1. An unconditional Citizen's Dividend would not awaken the personal responsibility that is a precondition for strengthening governance in favour of democracy. And under current deadweight tax policies it would not be possible to deliver a level of income that would make a material difference to people's welfare.

2. Fatally, the additional income channelled to all citizens would be absorbed in the land market. This would add to the burdens on low-income families who rent their homes. The evidence from Alaska is illuminating. It demonstrates what happens in the absence of the rent-as-public-revenue formula (Box 10.1).

Box 10.1 **Oil-rent dividend boosts house prices**

The Alaska Permanent Fund was created in 1979 by amendment to the Alaska Constitution to share the state's oil wealth. More than 640,000 Alaskans received a dividend of $1,884 in 2014, paid out of oil royalties. The annual pay-outs began in 1982. The largest dividend was $2,069 in 2008. An Alaskan who had received every dividend would have collected $37,027. Over its lifespan, the fund has paid out $22bn. There are no estimates of how much of the dividends actually remain in the pockets of citizens as discretionary spending power . Existing owners who sell their properties are able to anticipate that future dividends will increase the incomes of people moving into Alaska. So they increase the asking price of their homes, to capture – in advance – the future stream of oil rents. This leaves newcomers no better off: their dividends are committed to funding the higher mortgages on their homes.

Under the new financial algorithm, additional funds would become available for discretionary spending. The first tranche of those funds, however, would need to be dedicated to cultural renewal. The task, entailing years of commitment, would be to finance the clean-up of the damage created by the tax regime of past centuries.

▶ Victims of the killing cult would have the first claim on priority treatment. Tens of thousands of lives are at risk of premature termination in the UK alone. They lose upwards of a dozen years of what ought to be enjoyable retirement. We need a public index that measures the Years-of-Life-Lost. Publicity for that index would shame everyone and apply pressure on politicians. Parliamentarians who seek re-election would be asked: *Have your policies added to average life expectancy in places like Blackpool and Drumchapel?*

▶ Before distributing an unconditional, non-means-tested basic income to rich people, society would need to endow the families on low incomes so that they may enjoy enriched leisure years in retirement. Years in which they may give love to their families; plough energy back into the communities that succoured them; so that they may nurture nature through growing food or flowers on garden allotments; and nourish culture through engagement in artistic pursuits, sharing their wisdom and skills with the new generation.

Funds for the clean-up operation in other areas would be available to facilitate the transition to the Good Life.

- ▶ Infrastructure, such as highways and schools, need to be upgraded to benefit future generations as well as current users.

- ▶ Resources are needed to support people (particularly the elderly) who currently fund their care through capital gains.

- ▶ Culture needs to be rehabilitated, people's aesthetic sensibilities restored, the community's fabric repaired, the damaged environment healed.

The beauty of the financial algorithm is that all of these interventions would be self-funding. They increase the attractiveness of living in such environments. Productivity would be increased, rewarding society with an even higher net income. So there would come a point at which people could decide to invest part of the flow of rent to a sovereign wealth fund (to meet future needs) and to issue an annual Citizen's Rent Dividend.

A Citizen's Rent Dividend would serve a psychologically important political function. It would constantly remind the recipients that they were personally responsible for helping to create public value; and so they were entitled to a share of the nation's rents. Naming that dividend as *rent* would inspire people to remain alert. Rent-seeking, while it can be momentarily erased from culture, cannot be erased from our psyches. For as long as we remain sentient beings, rent-seeking will remain alive within all of us, ready to pounce when guards are dropped. The annual pay-out of a Citizen's Rent Dividend would be a permanent reminder for all of us to make sure that no-one was pilfering from the public purse. There are material rewards to be gained from fulfilling our responsibilities as custodians of good governance!

Everyone on the property ladder

Housing wealth in Britain is estimated at £4.5 trillion. That is one measure of the temptation that creates the evil which Churchill attempted to banish by reforming the public's finances.

The desire to enjoy the Easy Life drove early humans to find mutually beneficial solutions to the production and exchange of wealth. The earliest innovations generated the food surpluses that mitigated the uncertainties of the subsistence economy. From that point on, innovative genius took humans all the way to the moon. Things went wrong when some individuals were allowed to gain an unfair advantage over others by "getting on the property ladder.

The scramble to get on that ladder is understandable. The behaviour is driven by the belief that, if you are not climbing the ladder, you are a loser. That is why tenants remorsefully declare that paying rent is a waste of money (Box 10.2).

Box 10.2 **Stairways to Heaven?**

The payment of rent is not, in itself, the problem. Psychological dissonance arises from the awareness that tenants do not reap capital gains. To rub salt into their wounds, their rents fund the mortgages of buy-to-let investors who pocket all of the capital gains. Those gains are based on privileged treatment by irresponsible governance; privileges which tenants do not enjoy. It would be understandable if tenants sought a share of the capital gains that are accumulated during the period when they are paying their landlords' mortgages.

The inefficiencies and injustice embedded in home ownership were illustrated by research which revealed that elderly owners in Britain occupy over 8m properties worth £820bn which included 7.7m bedrooms that were unoccupied. The research was sponsored by Legal & General, the insurance company whose chief executive called on government to offer yet more tax privileges to elderly home-owners as bait to release their properties to families in need of homes.* Such tax breaks would be absorbed as higher land prices, further dislocating the housing market.

---

* Nigel Wilson (2015), "It's not just first-time buyers who need help in today's housing market", *Daily Telegraph*, June 1.

The property ladder symbolises the rent-seeking mission. The injustices of that culture can be erased without everyone owning the deeds to a house. The financial algorithm ensures that everyone shares the rents that are generated by rising productivity. This puts *everyone* on the property ladder.

Rent-sharing, achieved through access to the public services funded by rents, is the material pathway to a morally responsible society. No-one is condemned at birth to be a loser.

▶ Victors who now profit from the culture of cheating would not suffer material deprivation if they ceased to damage the lives of others.

▶ Victims of the culture of cheating would exchange the state of welfare dependency for the thrill of self-starting new lives of liberation.

Sharing the net income sets a new course for building relationships at all levels of association. It triggers the simultaneous reconstruction of personal identity, collective consciousness and the material fabric of communities. Renewal is a two-way process which overrides the magnetic pull of resources that converge on privileged people at the centre of power. Human synergy is maximised through the dynamic interactions that drive energy from the

▶ *bottom up:* no-one is excluded. Everyone contributes to collective well-being. This restores trust and nurtures culture as people go about their day-to-day affairs; and

▶ *top down:* power is driven down to all layers of decision-making. This reinforces stewardship towards the commons in all of its layers, in ways that nourish humanity.

A change in human nature is not required. All we need is the awareness of how rent-seeking inhibits us from even thinking about an authentic people-centred social system. We overcome the constraints on our minds by agreeing to negotiate a new social contract. That act of negotiation would engage everyone. In the process, it would serve as an exercise in collective therapy. It would animate the restoration of health to our collective consciousness.

All of this is achieved by the agreement to conform to one principle: *keep that portion of the value that you create by your labour, and share the public value which you work to create in cooperation with others.* That is the formula for human happiness. A happiness that would re-embark all of us on the mission that was launched by our ancestors: the evolution of humanity.

Epilogue

Beyond Democracy

IN a complex society, there are two primary information-discovering mechanisms. Both of ours are seriously impaired.

The first one has been the subject of this book: the pricing mechanism that is supposed to facilitate the funding of the services we share in common. In its present form, it is not administered as anything recognisable as a pricing mechanism. Its characteristics are those of arbitrariness, discrimination and abuse.

The second mechanism for determining people's wishes is the ballot box. But again, this is a seriously defective way of gauging people's authentic wishes. The succession of government policy disasters in recent decades in Britain were not willed by the people. So disconnected are they from the governing cliques that it is legitimate to ask whether anyone is governing the country. Two long-standing observers of Westminster politics conclude that, given the list of repetitive disasters, it is fair to say that no-one is at the political helm.[1]

If there was just one reason why people should have given democracy a chance to prove its worth, it was the need to restore the birthright to land. On that test, democracy has failed. But this was testimony to the vitality of the rent-seekers.

▶ At the end of the 19th century, the popular mood shifted in favour of a mandate for government to change the tax regime. The People's Budget (1909) sought to directly tax the nation's rents. Their lordships fought a desperate rearguard action.

Peers in the House of Lords found a way to despatch the law of the land. One of them, the Duke of Beaufort, declared: "I should like to see Winston Churchill and Lloyd George in the middle of 20 couple of dog hounds".[2]

▶ The policy was revived by Labour Chancellor of the Exchequer Philip Snowden in his 1931 Budget. Again, the rent-seekers prevailed. The Land Tax law was repealed in 1935 (Box E:1).

---

1 Ivor Crew and Anthony King (2013), *The Blunders of Our Government*, London: Oneworld; Anthony King (2015), *Who Governs Britain?* London: Pelican.
2 Budget League (2010), p.96.

Box E.1 **The manoeuvres of rent-seekers**

Austen Chamberlain orchestrated the Conservative Party's opposition to national land taxation from 1920-38. He formulated the Tory strategy in these Machiavellian terms:

"It is certain that if we do nothing the Radical Party will sooner or later establish their national tax, and once established in that form any Radical Chancellor...will find it an easy task to give a turn of the screw...On the other hand if this source of revenue...is once given to municipalities, the Treasury will never be able to put its finger in the pie again".*

Chamberlain's strategy proved effective. Today, the locally-administered property tax is regressive. It falls more heavily on low-value homes than on the high-value properties purchased for their asset value rather than as residences.

---

* Mason Gaffney (2004), "A Cannan Hits the Mark", in R.V. Andelson (ed.), *Critics of Henry George*, 2nd edn., Oxford: Blackwell Publishing, Vol. II.

And again, finally, democracy was put to the test in the 20 years following World War II. It came to nothing. These were all exercises in trying to reform the revenue system. If faith is to be restored in democracy, the litmus test is the return to this one issue: the rights and obligations with respect to the use of land and rent. Until we have confronted the failure to exercise our democratic rights, we have no right to advocate democracy to others, which is what western governments have been doing in Eastern Europe since 1991.

The culture of irresponsibility strangles the idea of democracy. The Mother of Parliaments mutated over the centuries to legitimise every step in the evolution of rent-seeking. Once the self-serving motives of this history are understood, the flaky behaviour of politicians becomes intelligible. They are not supposed to solve society's problems.

The architects of the values, laws and institutions of the Anglo version of politics were the agents of the most heinous crime against humanity imaginable. A feudal class that was destined to social obsolescence replaced their role as servants of the Crown with a culture of narcissism. To survive, so that it could continue to reap the nation's rents, that culture had to assume a life of its own. It had to be embalmed in the collective consciousness of the English people. To deal with the ever-present risk of opposition from the dispossessed, that culture had to take control of Parliament, to control the laws of the land. This was rent-seeking fossilised in a surreal theatre of the absurd.

One of the absurdities is the popular belief that Parliament *ought* to represent the best interests of the majority. But that was not the intent of those who fashioned the "unwritten constitution". Parliament, first and foremost, was fashioned as the guardian of a corrupt culture which survives on the misappropriation of socially-created income. Feudal monarchs ceased to represent the common interest when they lost fiscal power over the rents on which they relied to administer the affairs of State.

If the hijacking of the nation's rents does define a politicised culture of cheating, then we would expect to see the trademarks of that culture centre-stage in an event like the general election in May 2015. Sure enough, the fiscal system was used to manipulate people's voting intentions (see p.116). In exchange for votes, people were offered bribes in the form of new layers of unearned increments on top of the capital gains that would accrue to those who owned residential land. There was no declaration that the funds for those bribes would have to be extracted from resources hitherto devoted to the welfare of the sick and dependent parts of the population. That half of the equation came on June 22, 2015, when Prime Minister David Cameron announced changes to the tax regime (in the quest to find a further £12bn in cuts from the welfare budget). He announced the desire to move from a "low-wage, high-tax, high-welfare society to a higher-wage, lower-tax, lower-welfare society". The sponge effect of the land market would, in due course, translate the "reforms" into higher rents.

Corruption is now the systemic characteristic of western politics. Earned incomes are plundered by governments to sustain debt-based politics, while rents are at the mercy of whoever has the scheming intellect or muscle to grab them. Ultimately, corruption is at the expense of the nation's rents. An exponent of the naked variety is Greece (Box E:2). This came about because, back in history, the schemers disabled the immune system of an authentic democracy.

For people to exercise their freedoms at the point when they put crosses on ballot papers, they need two things. First, access to information. The openness of

---

Box E.2 **The systemic attack on corruption**

The use of bribery by Greek companies to corrupt foreign officials, according to the OECD, "sends an unfortunate message that foreign bribery is an acceptable means to win overseas business and improve Greece's economy during an economic crisis".[1]

The left-wing Syriza party erupted onto the Greek scene with the promise to clean up corruption. One of their targets was the "oligarchs" who exercised privileged access to the political system through ownership of the mass media. But corruption is sustained not by the moral weaknesses of individuals. It is enshrined in the character of the financial system.

Entrepreneurs cannot defray substantial bribes as a legitimate cost of business. Such payments would reduce returns on their working capital below market rates and render their firms uncompetitive. That is why bribes are ultimately at the expense of a nation's rents. If government will not collect that revenue, a free-for-all ensues. Those with the guile are free to dip their fingers in the pie. So corruption cannot be erased by the OECD's call for regulatory powers to investigate specific cases. To erase corruption at source it is necessary to remove the rents that tempt people into behaving badly.

As for Syriza, it secured power in the election of January 2015 by promising land owners that *they would abolish the property tax that fell on the rents of land!*[2]

---

1 OECD (2015), *Report on Implementing the Anti-Bribery Convention in Greece*, Paris.
2 Kerin Hope (2015), "Property tax backlash underpins Syriza's poll prospects", *Financial Times*, January 19.

the system – its transparency – shapes knowledge, and therefore the capacity to act in one's personal and social best interest. Secondly, the power to hold politicians responsible for their actions – accountability – depends on having an effective choice of candidates for office. But the power of money intervenes to control the selection of parties and candidates for high office.

Thus, the western brand of democracy is governance by a succession of failed politicians representing ideologies that ill-serve their constituents. The political process mimics what happens in the financial sector. As we saw in Chapter 3, when too-big-to-fail/gaol banks are caught out in public, they buy their way out of trouble. They pay a small chunk of their profits to one of the regulatory agencies as a fine "without admitting guilt". This is tokenism in accountability, a logical feature of the culture of cheating. Likewise with politics. Politicians who fail their people decline to accept guilt (Box E:3).

Box E.3 Guiltless politicians and clueless economists

Doctors are sworn to "do no harm" to their patients. No such oath is required of politicians. They may cause catastrophes when their hands are on the levers of power, but they walk away claiming to be guiltless. Thus, the Labour politicians who presided over the 2008 banking crisis in Britain displaced their personal responsibility by claiming that the cause had nothing to do with them. It was an "international financial crisis" over which they exercised no influence. Thus, their successors could seek election in 2015 claiming to have clean hands.

The politicians were aided by the academics, who almost unanimously asserted that the 2008 crisis was unpredictable. In Britain, typical was the claim by Richard Layard, a Labour peer and professor of economics at the London School of Economics. Gordon Brown's Labour government, he wrote, was the victim of "the worldwide financial crisis".[1] In the US, representative of this scholastic myopia was Lawrence Summers, Harvard professor of economics and a former US treasury secretary. He informed the World Economic Forum in Davos, Switzerland, in January 2015. "Nobody over the last 50 years, not the IMF, not the US Treasury, has predicted any of the recessions a year in advance, never".

Yet, in a book published in 1997, copies of which (with personal letters), were sent to Tony Blair and Gordon Brown when they took control of Downing Street and the UK Treasury, I forecast: "By 2007 Britain and most of the other industrially advanced economies will be in the throes of frenzied activity in the land market....Land prices will be near their 18-year peak....on the verge of the collapse that will presage the global depression of 2010".[2]

1 Richard Layard (2015), "It's a lie to say the Tories rescued Britain's economy", *The Times*, April 13.
2 Fred Harrison (2007), *The Chaos Makers*, 1997: Vindex, p.27.

But does this mean that democratic governance is beyond redemption? What are the alternatives? If the democratic system is to be rehabilitated, honesty about its origins is the starting point. The two most elaborately constructed versions in history were funded out of rents that were produced by slaves.

▶ The template model, from classical Athens, was funded by the rents from the silver mines of Laurium. Those mines were worked by slaves.

▶ The Anglo version was funded out of rents generated from two primary sources. The first was the labour of the dispossessed, the peasants who produced the rural rents of England but were deprived of their share of that revenue. The second was from the purchase and transportation of slaves from Africa for sale in the Americas; plus the rents from the plantations, some of which found its way back into the purchase of real estate in England.

Advocates of western values argue that, while not perfect, democracy is better than the alternatives. That is special pleading of a pathetic kind. We may examine its logic in relation to the two globally significant social transformations in our lifetime.

▶ **The Soviet Union** imploded when a critical mass of people turned up in their town squares and demanded western-style democracy. Western governments and think-tanks moved in to help shape new institutions and laws. They advocated the formal trappings of democracy, but their overriding intent was the privatisation of state assets, including land and natural resources. The winners were the oligarchs. In Russia, the average age of middle class professionals slumped by five years under the trauma of the "shock doctrine" that rationalised the Grand Larceny.[3]

▶ **Muslim countries** saw tyrannical rule overthrown during the Arab Spring which began in 2011. Again, the popular narrative was framed by the imported doctrines of democracy. The West, under the guise of helping to establish new institutions, reinforced the power of the elites to make sure that property rights remained in private hands. This included the ownership of land held by the military in, for example, Egypt; where the first popularly elected president was quickly overthrown by the army.

In these two epochal events, the State-building agenda was camouflage for enshrining the rent-seeking model. The ensuing suffering continues to this day, more than 20 years after the collapse of communism, as I saw at close quarters in Bosnia in 2014 (Box E:4).

The outcome is endemic corruption and the consolidation of a corrosive cynicism directed at the concept of democracy. But is there a viable alternative to the West's version of democracy? For many people, that question is heretical. Even more uncomfortable is the answer that can be constructed from the history of the two economies at the top of the Index of Economic Freedom. They achieved the top slots because of clean commercial practices, security of property, low taxes and the efficiency of their markets.

---

3 Fred Harrison (2008), *The Silver Bullet*, London: theIU, p.25.

Box E.4 **Bosnia's experiment in participative democracy**

ASSET privatisation in Eastern Europe led to the gutting of economically viable enterprises as a new class of "investors" stripped assets and sold the land to speculators. Territories that were rich in labour skills and natural resources collapsed into poverty.

In Bosnia and Herzegovina, angry citizens took to the streets in protest in February 2014. Government buildings were burnt down. As passions calmed, people gathered in what turned out to be a unique exercise in participative democracy. In each town, plenums convened in which citizens set the agenda and appointed their moderators. A conscious decision was made to avoid a hierarchical organisation. This obliged the participants to accept that they could not shift personal responsibilities onto others (the "leaders"). Plenum meetings ended when the country suffered devastating spring floods. At the time of writing (June 2015) they have not reconvened.

Meanwhile, the oligarchs are safeguarding their financial fortunes by locking their cash into top-end real estate in the capitals of Western Europe.

▶ **No. 1 is Hong Kong.** It enjoys "an efficient regulatory framework, low and simple taxation, and sophisticated capital markets". No-one is told, however, that Hong Kong was the British colony whose land was made available exclusively on leasehold terms. Rents were paid into the public purse to fund some of the best infrastructure and public housing services in the world, alongside the lowest tax rates on earned incomes. This outcome was built on governance that did not rest on the popular vote. It was a model of civil service administration supervised by the Foreign and Commonwealth Office in London.

▶ **No. 2 is Singapore.** "[This] society has a low tolerance for corruption, and the effective rule of law strongly undergirds all aspects of economic development". After achieving independence from Britain, Singapore was ruled by Lee Kwan Yew with an "iron fist". According to the BBC's obituary, Lee was criticised "for his iron grip on power. Under him freedom of speech was tightly restricted and political opponents were targeted by the courts". Lee gave priority to value-adding entrepreneurs. Rent-seeking was disallowed. Compensation to owners whose land was acquired for public purposes was set at agricultural land values. This meant that the rental values that rose as a result of public investments went into the public purse. Today, about 90% of Singapore's land is publicly owned, tax rates are low, and people's incomes are among the highest in the world.

The top ratings repeatedly awarded to these two economies are not biased by leftist ideology. The Index is compiled by the right-wing Washington DC-based Heritage Foundation and the *Wall Street Journal.*[4]

---

4 http://www.heritage.org/index/

We could add further examples of how prosperity and security are not contingent on western-style democracy. Taiwan is an important example. When Chairman Mao finally triumphed over Sun Yat-sen's Kuomintang (KMT) and drove its army off mainland China, refuge was sought on the island of Formosa. There, the KMT pensioned off the rural landlords under a "land-to-the-tiller" programme, established an urban land value tax in 1954 and created the first Asian Tiger.

What mattered to the people of Hong Kong, Singapore and Taiwan was not so much the formal veneer of democracy as the freedom to earn a better life for themselves and their children. The theme common to these and other similar examples is the low incidence of abusive taxation, made possible by important elements of a *democratised financial system*. The personal and direct responsibility to fund public services out of rents turned these communities into the most productive in the world. We cannot pronounce them as heavens on earth. There were, and are, flaws in these models; but would the people who valued the liberation of their labours have traded these systems for the constitutional rights available to the citizens of democratic Bosnia? I don't think so!

This evidence, however, does not amount to an argument against democracy *per se*. The disengagement from politics of people within the democracies of the West has reached emergency levels. Apathy and vitriolic cynicism render western nations vulnerable to malevolent forces from extremes of both Left and Right. Politically (and not just economically), Europe has transported itself back to the chaos of the 1930s. But the continent's statesmen do not question either the founding principles of the model of politics which they inherited, or their role in perpetuating practises that succour the culture of cheating.

From all the evidence we have compiled, we must conclude that the only viable solution is to be found in the synthesis of the universal franchise with an amended code of practice. This must take the form of the personal responsibility to democratise the rents from all sources. The appeal for a bold response to the economic crisis from the *Financial Times* endorses this view. While Britain's politicians were horse-trading during the 2015 election campaign, the *Financial Times* reviewed the dismal productivity of the UK economy and concluded that new measures were needed, especially in the realm of land taxation. Pessimistically, however, it added:

> "Delivering these would prove just as fraught as when David Lloyd George and Winston Churchill tried to take on landed interests a century ago. But decades of stagnant growth are a much worse prospect."[5]

The culture of irresponsibility has now enjoyed a further century in which to consolidate its power over people's minds. Despair is entrenched, as attested by the repeated observations by Martin Wolf, the chief economics commentator of the *Financial Times*. In discussing the socially crippling consequences of

---

5 *Financial Times* (2015), "UK's weak productivity invites a bolder response", April 22.

inequality, he reminds his readers that the taxation of land was "politically difficult".[6] This is the crisis of democracy. In a society that enshrines the right of the individual to liberty, people are constrained from acting in their best personal and common interests, even as their hands are poised with pencils over the ballot papers in the privacy of the voting booth. Why? Psychiatrist Thomas Lewis and his colleagues offer an explanation from neuroscience:

"Steeped as they are in limbic physiology, healthy people have trouble forcing their minds into the unfamiliar outline of this reptilian truth: no intrinsic restraint on harming people exists outside the limbic domain."[7]

The significance of this insight was noted in Chapter 6. Low-income families rear their infants under conditions which damage the limbic part of the brain. This impairs the emotions that nurture their relationships with others, and the capacity to empathise with the common good. What chance is there of reform if the people with the most to gain have been assaulted into complying with, and therefore preserving, the culture that damages their own lives? And as for those of us who own (albeit minuscule) plots of land that yield astonishing capital gains, what chance is there of reason prevailing over self-interest?

These questions bring us to two concluding reflections. The first concerns the time available to effect change. Increasingly, we hear voices suggesting that the West faces an existential threat. As I have sought to show, the major threat is from within, a conclusion that provokes many questions.

Did previous civilisations implode because people failed to ostracise the culture of cheating? The financial wires in our civilisation are entangled into one unwholesome mess. Might the crisis of 2008 be the wake-up call that mobilises a democratic consensus behind an authentic financial reform? We cannot sensibly answer that question without an understanding of what drove the rise and fall of civilisations since the first terminal catastrophes in antiquity. We shall address these questions in the second volume of this trilogy.

But a further major puzzle remains to be unravelled. *Where has God been these past few centuries?* That question imposed itself as I researched the fate of nearly 800 infants and children who died while in the care of Catholic nuns. The deaths occurred over a 35-year period in post-colonial Ireland. Falling pregnant out of wedlock invited social disgrace. "Fallen women" were given shelter at the St Mary's Mother and Baby Home. But after one year, mother was wrenched from child. The women were despatched to lives of anguish, not knowing the fate of their offspring. The children, their limbic brains atrophied, were drilled in dormitories in what was originally built as a workhouse for the destitute. The rupture of the maternal bond was emotional castration inflicted on infants by the sisters of Jesus who dangled the crucifix around their necks. The infants were starved of the milk of love.

---

6 Martin Wolf (2015), "A world of difference", *Financial Times*, May 2.
7 Lewis *et. al.* (2000), p.216.

The psychobiological immune systems of those infants were so weakened that they were especially vulnerable to disease or famine. They were buried in unmarked graves in a back yard in a small town in County Galway, unprotected by either the power of the sacred or the secular power of democracy. The third volume in our interrogation of the human condition will consider whether we should continue to abide by one of the cheating culture's key strictures: separate politics from religion.

Appendix

Mortgaging Your Life

REALITY unfolds with clarity when we talk our way through the purchase of a house. The average price of a property in Scotland in January 2015 was £160,000, according to the Nationwide Building Society. At the time, Nationwide's 5-year fixed mortgage was 4.9% APR. Assume that, to buy such a house, you put down a deposit of £10,000, and you make up the difference of £150,000 with a mortgage, repayable over 25 years. The monthly redemption payment on your pledge to create a value of £150,000 over the course of 25 years was £929.21. The annual outlay is £11,150. Over 25 years, that amounts to a total of £278,763. Thus, the interest on the "loan" – the money which Nationwide did not give you – is £128,763.

Nationwide did authenticate your claim that you were in employment and that your wages were sufficient to cover the monthly outgoings on your IOU. Furthermore, it holds the deeds to the property in safe keeping for 25 years. Therefore, it was entitled to a fee. But did it *earn* £128,763 for that service?

Exactly what is the nature of that value which is classified as *interest* on the mythical loan?

The agreed price of the house was £160,000. This was the value which the vendor placed on his property, under the market conditions that prevailed at the time of sale. That value included the cost of the bricks and mortar of the building, plus the attributes of the location. The value you placed on this particular location is subjective. Your preferences might include access to a good hospital, or a school with a high reputation, or the availability of public parks and transport systems linking the locality with centres of employment. Such preferences vary from one family to another. Nonetheless, with the benefit of the market, individual preferences are compared to establish the best price for that locality's house *and* the social amenities in its catchment area. The purchaser is the bidder who places the highest value on those amenities, and is willing to pay for them.

The winning bid includes the realisation that an additional £128,763 will have to be deducted from earnings. This assumes that the "interest" rate remained the same over the 25-year period. Historically, the long-run rate of interest has been

5%, so our hypothetical case is close to reality.

What would happen if, say, government passed a law which made it possible to borrow money free of interest? One thing is certain: that £128,763 would not remain in your pocket. Why? Because the vendor would be aware that the financial go-between was no longer going to collect such a large slice of your future earnings. Therefore, through the marketplace, that sum would be added to the selling price of the house. And because you can afford to pay that higher price, you agree to do so.

All the bargaining cards are in the hands of the vendor. That is because the supply of dwellings in the area where you want to live is fixed. And the reason for that is obvious: land is fixed in supply. *The increase in the price of the property is not attributable to the bricks and mortar, which are depreciating with every passing day.* That £128,763 is merged into the value of the land.

Index

Adam Smith Institute,130-131
Ahern, Berti, 75
Alaska Permanent Fund, 139
Anglo Irish Bank, 70
Argyle, Duke of, 59
Aristocracy, 20, 24, 25, 52, 55, 59, 61, 110
 - primogeniture and, 29, 54, 63
 - rent-seeking and, 56-57, 63
Astor, 4th Viscount, 110, 122
ATCOR thesis, 16, 17, 19, 94, 11, 113, 133, 137-139

Bacon, Peter, 69
Bank of Ireland Private Banking,
Banks, 45, 47, 146
 - as rent appropriators, 43, 126
 - money creation and, 38, 40-44, 126-128, 153-154
 - 2008 crisis and, 39, 42, 44, 66-67, 90, 127
Barclays Bank, 45
Beaufort, Duke of, 143
Bentham, Jeremy, 13
Berelowitz, Sue, 87
Blair, Tony, 38, 63, 64, 89-91, 146
Bosnia, 130, 147-149
Bradford, 82
Brown, Gordon, 38, 146
Bruce, Robert the, 108
Bruton, John, 75
Burke, Edmund, 77-78
Burke, Ray, 74
Burns, Harry, 84
Butler, Eamonn, 131

Cable, Vince, 44
Callely, Ivor, 74
Cameron, David, 44, 46, 95, 110, 116-118, 145
Carney, Mark, 39
Chamberlain, Austen, 144
Cheating
 - capital gains and, 60
 - civilisation and, 150-151
 - cultural process, 1, 2, 8, 18, 21, 32, 51-52, 87, 96, 102, 107, 133-134, 149
 - financial sector and, 33, 35, 39, 45, 47, 124, 146
 - rent and, 5, 141, 145
See also: Consciousness, collective; Ireland; David Cameron;
Churchill, W.S., 1-4, 79, 140, 143
Citizen's Rent Dividend, 140
Clooney, George, 70
Clooney, Nicholas, 70
Cobden, Richard, 18
Collective consciousness,
Common good, 5, 30, 81, 94, 134, 135, 150
Commons, 8, 25, 30, 54, 85, 86, 142
 - defined 6, 77

 - personality and, 7, 53
See: England.
Commons, House of, 1-2, 18, 71, 90
Comte, August, 23, 24
Consciousness, collective, 4, 6, 33, 77, 142
 - cheating and, 60, 73, 131
 - rents and, 53, 87, 141, 144
Corn Laws, 23, 58
Crotty, Richard, 68
Culture, 6, 8, 30, 31, 51-64, 81-83, 85, 86, 97, 124, 140
 - bankers and, 35-36, 39, 44-45, 47, 93
 - cheating and, 1, 5, 18, 32, 87, 96, 102, 116, 123, 128, 133-134, 145, 146, 149-150
 - rent-seeking and, 19, 24, 33, 40, 51-53, 79, 88, 90, 107, 109, 119, 138, 144
 - social pathology and, 3
 - suppressed, 7, 52
See: Commons; Killing Cult; Ireland

D:Ream, 89
Darwin, Charles, 13, 24, 25, 30
David I, 108
Davitt, Michael, 71
Deeter, Karl, 65
Denmark, 20
Downshire, Lord, 72
Dublin, 65, 66, 68-69, 71-76
Durham, Bishop of, 81

East India Company, 78
Economist, The, 15, 20, 21, 23
Egypt, 147
Elizabeth II, 91, 116
England, 22, 54, 62, 73
 - child abuse in, 87
 - class ideology in, 52, 60
 - common rights and, 1-2
 - commons of, 25, 57, 80, 128
 - culture of greed and, 72
 - institutional corruption in, 86-87
 - premature deaths in, 83-84
 - rents of, 5, 113-115, 147
 - Single Tax and, 14
England, Bank of, 13, 15, 29, 36, 37, 39-40, 124, 125
English Heritage, 54
European Central Bank, 75
Evil, 1, 4, 5, 118, 124
 - W.S Churchill defines, 3, 140
 - G.W. Norman and, 13
 - H. Spencer and, 26-27
Evolution,
 - English state and, 52, 55
 - human, 5, 7, 98, 142
 - social, 6, 24-26, 30, 85, 108, 123, 135, 144

Feudalism, 107, 109
Financial Times, The, 19, 20, 60, 65, 70, 74, 82, 98-99, 127, 149
Flat tax, 128-131
Forsey, Frederick, 74
Frame, Robin, 70

Gaffney, Mason, 29, 102, 112, 138
George, David Lloyd, 4, 143, 149
George, Henry, 28, 29, 71
Glasgow, 83-84, 123
Greece, 76, 90-91, 95, 107, 108, 145
Green, Stephen, 46-47
Guardian, The, 46

Happiness, 6, 14, 19, 23, 30, 124
  - financial algorithm and, 13, 125, 142
  - rent and, 15
See: G.W. Norman; H. Spencer.
Harris, Anne, 76
Haughey, Charlie, 74
Henry VIII, 18, 55
Heritage Foundation, 66, 148
Hitler, Adolf, 125, 126
HM Treasury, 13, 38, 63, 64, 112, 138, 144, 146
Hong Kong, 66, 129-130, 148, 149
Housing,
Housing, 93, 131
  - benefits, 88
  - bubble, 75
  - buy-to-let, 60, 141
  - capital gains and, 88, 138, 140
  - cheating and, 118, 141
  - costs of, 26, 63, 88-89, 98-99
  - ladder, 19, 117
  - market, 32, 35, 42, 66, 69, 88, 89, 141
  - social, 31, 117, 130, 148
  - taxation and, 64
HSBC, 46-47
Hudson, Michael, 101
Hughes, Stuart, 29
Humanity, 6, 9, 79, 85-86, 107, 135, 142, 144
  - defined, 7, 30, 133
  - evils and, 26
  - rent and, 3, 5, 8, 21, 51, 98
  - unified theory of, 133
Hurstfield, Joel, 52, 62
Hutton, Will, 33

Iceland, 127
India, 63, 78
Individualism, 54-55, 102
Institute for Fiscal Studies, 85, 117, 119
Ireland, 20, 66,
  - as Celtic Tiger, 66
  - banks and, 69
  - child deaths in, 150-151
  - culture of greed and, 72, 76
  - European Union and, 73
  - George Osborne on, 65
  - Green Party 76
  - housing and, 67
  - land taxes and, 71
  - land values in, 69-70
  - migration and, 72
  - property tax and, 67

Jamaica, 121, 123
James IV, 108
James VI, 108
Johnson, Boris, 31-32
Journal, Wall Street, 66, 148
Jupp, Sir Kenneth, 1, 2

Kay, John, 40
Kerrigan, Gene, 74, 75
Kill Zone: see Killing Cult
Killally, Gwer, 74
Killing cult, 26, 51, 80, 83-84, 139
  - babies and, 79
  - culture and, 85-87, 107, 123
  - kill zone, 82
  - rent and, 89
King, Mervyn, 39, 40
Krugman, Paul, 33, 100-102

Land, 2, 7, 27, 53, 60, 62, 102, 115
  - bubbles and, 36, 67, 127, 131, 146
  - grabs, 28, 35, 36, 56, 58, 61, 73, 81, 96, 98-99, 110, 118, 123
  - market, 17, 19, 21, 37, 63, 68, 90, 95, 127, 139
  - owners, 3-4, 19, 21, 30, 36, 56, 58, 61, 73, 81, 96, 98-99, 110, 118, 123
  - property rights in, 24-25, 27-29, 35, 54, 57, 59, 70-72, 80, 143, 147, 148
  - rent of, 15, 16, 18, 31, 36, 45, 58, 94, 96, 101, 111, 114, 125, 127, 144, 145
  - speculation in, 59, 69, 73, 76, 85, 99, 102, 123, 125, 130, 148
  - stewardship of, 6, 109-110
  - sustainability and, 115
  - value of, 4, 5, 19, 20, 42, 60, 68-69, 74, 88, 109, 117, 119, 141, 148, 154
See also: H. George; P. Krugman; OECD; Scotland; H. Spencer
Laslett, Peter, 60
Lawlor, Liam, 74
Laxton, Notts.,54
Layard, Richard, 146
Legal & General, 141
Lenihan, Brian, 69
Lewis, Thomas, 150
Little, Dorothy, 121-122
Little, Simon, 121
Locke, John, 16
Lucan, Lord, 72

Magna Carta, 1-2
Mahon, Alan, 73
Mao, Tse-tung, 149
Marquand, David, 2, 4
Marshall, Alfred, 4, 53, 96, 133
Marx, Karl, 62, 124
Miliband, Ed, 33

Mill, J.S., 13, 102
Miller, G.J., 83
Money, 35, 37, 46-47, 53, 57, 74, 88-89, 119, 124
 – corruption and, 52, 74, 146
 – property and, 38, 45, 59, 110, 141
Morgan, J.P., 44
Moriarty, Michael, 73
Mugabe, Robert, 110

NASA, 102
New York Times, 44, 100,
Nonconformist, 23
Norman, G.W., 17, 20-23, 29, 36, 37, 124-125
 – happiness and, 13-15, 18-19
North Dakota, Bank of, 127

O'Brien, Francie, 74
O'Cofaigh, Eoin, 69
OECD, 26, 66-67, 145
Office of National Statistics, 26, 117, 119
Osborne, George, 65, 66, 119

Padoan, Pier Carlo, 66-67
Parnell, Charles Stewart, 71
Paul, Diane, 30
Pembroke, Lord, 71
People's Budget, The, 4, 71, 143
Pickard, Duncan, 109, 111
Picketty, Thomas, 5
Portland, Duke of, 78
Powell, Jonathan, 89
Price, Bonamy, 22
Psychosis, 6, 35-37, 39-40, 134
Public value, 57, 97, 118, 130, 140, 142
 – Alfred Marshall and, 4, 53, 96, 133
 – appropriation of, 55, 62, 108, 138
See: Rent

Quinn, Frank, 65

Rabushka, Alvin, 128-130
Reagan, Ronald, 96
Redmond, John, 71
Rent, 7-8, 16-17, 21, 37, 45, 70-71, 80, 88-89, 97-98, 100-102, 114, 117, 118, 124, 127, 135, 141
 – cheating and, 5, 22, 78
 – compensation and, 31, 121-123
 – economic rent, 4, 26, 40, 111
 – happiness and, 15
 – humanity and, 5
 – interest as, 42
 – privatisation and, 8, 27, 36, 54, 82-83, 102
 – taxation and, 17-20, 24, 28-29, 76, 128, 136, 141
See: ATCOR; Citizen's Rent Dividend; England; Public Value; Rent-seeking; Scotland
Rentenmark, 125
Rent-seeking, 19, 24, 28-29, 33, 35, 36, 40, 44-45, 51-64, 72, 79, 81, 87, 90, 99, 107, 109, 111, 116, 119, 128, 134-135, 142-144, 147, 148
Ricardo, David, 16, 32, 94, 100-102
Ricardo's Law, 32, 83
Robertson, James, 128

Rogers, J.E. Thorold, 21-22
Rubinstein, W.D., 58, 59
Russia, 147
Rutland, Earl of, 54

Saltaire, 82
Schacht, W.L., 125
Scotland, 70, 100, 123
 – banks and, 109-110
 – housing and, 42, 115
 – land reform and, 107, 109-111, 115, 122
 – rents and, 107, 109, 115
 – taxation and, 111-115
Scotland, Royal Bank of, 44
Scottish Land and Estates, 123
Scottish National Party, 110, 111, 113, 115, 122
Shelter (charity), 88
Singapore, 66, 148, 149
Slavery, 121-123, 146-147
Smith, Adam, 16, 24, 94, 95, 102, 124, 130, 131
Snowden, Philip, 143
Social galaxy, 57, 85, 133-134
Sociology, 7, 23, 24, 27, 31, 53
Spain, 76
Spectator, The, 15
Spencer, Herbert, 28-32
 – happiness and, 23, 26-27
Stern, Sir Nicholas, 63, 64
Stewardship, 6, 43, 73, 124, 135-136, 142
Stiglitz, Joseph, 33
Summers, Lawrence, 146
Sun Yat-sen, 149
Syriza (party), 145

Taiwan, 149
Taxation, 4, 14, 16-18, 73, 148-149
 – deadweight losses from, 15, 63-64, 112
 – economic rent and, 40, 144
 – ethics of, 20, 131
 – land and, 15, 16, 18, 20. 28, 64, 71, 86, 95, 111, 124, 143-144, 149-150
 – premature deaths and, 83
See: H. George; G.J. Miller; G.W. Norman; H. Spencer.
Taylor, Frank, 76
Thatcher, Margaret, 31, 33, 96
Thompson, E.P., 52, 61
Thornberry, Emily, 117
Thurley, Simon, 54
Treanor, Jill, 46
Trust, 5, 7, 41, 66, 124-128, 141

UN Declaration of Human Rights, 47
United Nations, 32, 47, 102

Vesci, Lord de, 71

West, Geoffrey, 94-95
Wightman, Andy, 108
Wilberforce, W., 121
Wolf, Martin, 19-20, 124-125

Yew, Lee Kwan, 148